Into the Light

Into the Light

A Novel by

Alex Hancock

Donald S. Ellis · Publisher

Creative Arts Book Company
1985

The characters and events described in this book are entirely fictitious. Any resemblances to persons living or dead are coincidental.

Published by Donald S. Ellis, and distributed by Creative Arts Book Company.
For information contact:
Creative Arts Book Company
833 Bancroft Way
Berkeley, California 94710

ISBN 0-916870-99-5 (cloth)
I3DN 0-916870 98 7 (paper)

Library of Congress Catalog Card No. 84-72413

The publication of this book was supported in part by a grant from the National Endowment for the Arts in Washington, D.C., a Federal Agency.

Contents

Author's Note

The game that Dwight and Hazard see in Chapter 1 did not take place at Wrigley Field on August 27, 1962. Even if it had, Al Heist could not have caught the final out—he was with Houston by then—and Jack Spring could not have yielded the grand-slam homer: his brief visit to the Cubs took place in 1964.

Though the city of Chicago might one day name its schools after former Cub player-managers, neither an Anson Elementary nor a Grimm High has so far existed there.

Any person who attempted to use this book as a guide to the streets and the commercial landmarks of a particular neighborhood on the North Side of Chicago would soon be lost.

1.   Wrigley Field, August 27, 1962

We come early. We'll stay late, or forever.

Get off the el and come down the wooden steps and even before touching Addison Street get hit in the face by the smell of the ballpark. The smell alone would say This is it even if a person had gone blind and couldn't see the sunlight falling through the el tracks onto the street and the stand where the bald guy with a red moustache sells team pennants and the rest of his junk.

The game starts one-thirty. Me and the boy get here before eleven. To watch batting practice. To turn red, dry, hoarse. We come to bask in the smoke of a hundred cigars.

I try to walk slow down Sheffield the long block from the el to the bleacher gate but still the old man can't keep up so he sends me on ahead, "Hurry and get seats in the front row." Which is a laugh since we'll be about the first ones in the bleachers. Sixty-eight last April and he walks bent enough that nobody would know he stands a good two inches taller than me. For as long as I've known him he's walked bent, his years in the mine must have made him this way but he never talks to me about the mine. Maybe he goes off into the old days when he talks to himself. While I'm in the kitchen trying to fix something edible on hot evenings I hear his voice from the bedroom, too quiet to catch the words.

Already hot. Already I can tell the only wind today will come from the south. The dry wind that makes me wonder why I bother trying to take a breath.

Let Dwight walk on. No point slowing him down. Burdening him with what my lungs know. In a year or so I will make him more of an orphan than he already is. Meantime, no pity. If I cough black blood smoking my White Owl of an evening, I cough into a rag.

Pushing through the turnstile the smell comes to you even sharper, as if your quarters pay for the smell as much as the ballgame. Tommy Rigney still comes here for the smell alone and the sounds of the crowd, letting the radio tell him what he'll never see. In the middle of the smell is the smoke of cigars, around the edges mustard and hotdogs, popcorn, and circling everything—shut your eyes for it—beer. By the middle of a long game the right-field bleachers get to smelling soaked in beer, and this game is bound to be long because the wind's blowing out from home, innings so long you start sweating beer and cigar smoke.

I don't smoke much because who wants to stunt their growth, not that I tower over anybody anyway, being at five-seven-and-a-quarter one of the smaller guys in the Class of '63 at Grimm, but two months ago on the night of my sixteenth birthday I heisted one of his White Owls. It made me dizzy all night, lying there wondering how a thing that's supposed to make you feel like a man could make you feel more like a kid.

In a way I'm lucky. Say the Depression had never hit. Say the mine never closed. I would have been below for good. There right now, assuming I hadn't already died one way or the other. Instead I made it to Chicago. Worked other jobs. Tried to raise a daughter. Tried to raise her son. Got to take him to Wrigley Field a few dozen times.

The mine is killing me, after all, you could call me luckier than some.

Every time I come up the cool ramp and step out into the open stands above the outfield all the shades of green make me stop. The rows of long benches are painted a dark shining green which keeps peeling away to show paler and paler greens. People who sat here when these faded greens were dark saw Babe Ruth point from home to the centerfield bleachers and then homer to the exact spot, if he really did point, which nobody knows for sure which probably makes it a legend.

The Babe called his shot on October 1st, 1932, according to the Baseball Encyclopedia in the branch library on Racine which happens to be an excellent place to go do homework after school. Nineteen thirty-two, in the days when grampa first started coming out here. But he never saw the Babe. How could he have bought a ticket for the World Series?

Halfway up the ramp, this little sign on the wall in red letters: NO GAMBLING. In these bleachers I've heard men gamble if the next pitch will be a ball or a strike.

Never use to gamble. Now I do. When I started up this ramp, gambled I'd make it to the top. And won.

Use to be we'd walk all the way to the ballpark. No need to ride the el two stops. Now there's a need.

Stand still. Find the boy.

Already the waves of heat, rising from the diamond.

There. Front row near the right-field corner. The skinny frame. Dark hair. Us Harkers were a fair lot. Got his dark features from his worthless bum of a father.

Keep moving. Wait. One more breath.

Some people call this place God's Country. Dumbness. Too much talk of God. Men made Wrigley Field. Men, working.

Arriving this early you find a sort of quiet that gets eaten by the crowd later on. Close your eyes and it sounds as weird as lying on the beach with the waves and the lifeguard's whistle seeming far away. Vada Pinson comes gliding back this way for a fungo and even though I'm leaning across the wall right above him I can barely hear the slap of the ball into his glove, but the bat meeting the ball sounds loud and sharp from three hundred sixty-eight feet.

The ivy is an even more perfect green than the outfield grass until you look close and see it's beginning to turn brown, just in time for the start of school. At least no more old bimbo Spensely for English this fall, the Wicked Witch of the Midwest. Write about a colorful character, she told us one Friday last winter, come in Monday with a short essay on someone who qualifies as colorful. After class Jerry Garth asked me was I going to use my grandfather. Jerry had only met Hazard once but that time the old man told some dumb joke and sat there in the rocker slapping his knee so Jerry decided he must be colorful.

My grandfather is not colorful, my grandfather is just himself, old, an old workhorse who fixed it with the foreman so he could keep working past retirement, an old Cub fan for half his life who still takes me to Wrigley Field to see them keep stinking out the joint year after year. Hazard Harker, who loves the green ivy turning brown by the end of the season.

All around, boys my own age or younger, some here in groups, some with their fathers. The only one here with his grandfather: me. If I still had a father I wouldn't be here with him anyway unless they moved Wrigley Field to Arizona or wherever he is. Hell, maybe he's nowhere near Arizona, maybe he's right here at Wrigley Field right now. I wouldn't even recognize him, at least not by his face, but maybe you can recognize a person you used to know by the feeling you'd get from their being a few rows back of you at Wrigley Field.

If he had his hands over his face. His face covered by his hands. Was that a time?

If I still had a mother she'd bring me here if I asked her. Whoever she would have turned out to be.

But nowadays I pay my own way.

Once in a while the kid will stare at nothing. Just now, staring into the ivy. Never says what's on his mind. Fine. Let him keep his secrets. I can rattle on whether he listens or no.

"You know what's different here?"

"What's different, Grampa?"

"Other ballparks have got advertising. Big signs on the outfield wall. Let's say you go to the ballgame to forget everything. Make the world disappear a few hours. You can't do it. All around you the signs keep bringing the world back. Wear this. Drink that. Buy now pay later. Look around here. No such signs at Wrigley. Here we look at nothing but the players. Our scorecards. The grass, the ivy. The scoreboard. Here we worry about nothing. Except how in damnation the Cubs will manage to lose another."

As usual he orders two, one for himself right now, the other for me to take sips from while he finishes the first.

"Go easy." What does he mean, go easy, does he think I'm a teenage lush? He's the one should take it easy with the beer, he's not exactly in his prime taking a week to walk one block, mumbling the same old stuff about nothing but ivy on the walls of Wrigley Field. And when he takes a breath he sounds like sawing through prison bars. Go easy! Half the time I can't figure out what this man means and the other half he doesn't talk. Never a word how he feels, no tales of his years in the mine, never says if my mother went to the beach on days like this or preferred hiding from the sun. He never even told me where she's buried. When you're grown up I'll tell you where, he says.

And he gets to decide when I'm grown up?

Now what? Can't we even come to the ballgame in peace. All of a sudden this man in a White Sox hat is telling Dwight to shut his you-know-what trap. Fine way to talk in front of his own boy.

"He kicked me in the back," Dwight says to the White Sox hat, "he can say excuse me."

The kid did kick me in the back, even if he didn't mean to. But his father just gives me a hate look. "My boy doesn't have to say a thing to you. You can drop dead." Meanwhile the kid himself is hiding his face behind his scorecard till I'm ready to rip it out of his hands and make him at least look at me but then of all things Hazard speaks up.

"You'd better watch how you address my grandson, young man."

Now this jerk in the White Sox hat must be thirty years younger than Hazard and a hell of a lot stronger when you figure in the old man being so tired lately but something in the way my grandfather speaks those words makes the guy back off.

"Okay," the guy says. "Okay. We're all here for a good time."

For those few words all the tiredness went out of Hazard's voice, leaving him free and strong enough to speak his mind in a way that forced you to pay attention. Forced you to watch how you addressed his grandson.

Can't even watch batting practice in peace. Or leave trouble behind.

I want to thank Hazard for sticking up for me but how do I say it, and anyway he's gone back to checking his scorecard against the players: "Robinson. Frank Robinson this one must be. He's the one leans a little bit over the plate. Like a man waiting for a subway. You ever notice when this Robinson's up to bat?"

"He does," I say. "He leans a bit."

He's right. The way Frank Robinson leans forward does resemble a man peering down the tunnel. I still want to thank him.

The White Sox hat could be my father, any dark-haired man around age forty in Wrigley Field today could be. Or watching a minor league game in Phoenix, Denver, Sacramento, for all I know.

You get to be this way. Mark your life by the troubles you left behind when you came to a certain ballgame. That godawful long day out here against the Giants. What Brickhouse calls a Pier Six Brawl. Game lasted close to five hours. After, stopped at Smalley's for one last Old Style. People couldn't believe it: What a game! One more inning it would have got called for darkness. By the time I got home night had fallen. In the hallway, tried to make sense of this Western Union wire. Arizona. The Highway Patrol, or was it State Police? It took me a long time, in the dark hall.

Now I mark the start of a whole part of my life by that game. Those shadows growing longer over the field while the Cubs went down in the fourteenth.

Meeting the kid, too. Train ride lasted so long I got afraid the rye would dry up inside the flask. Bare, tired country. then face to face with a five-year-old stranger in a small town station. He didn't look like any kin of mine. I could not think of one thing to say.

"I'm taking you back to Chicago, Dwight," I finally said. "Where the Cubs play baseball."

The kid didn't even know who the Cubs were yet. What did he care, hearing those words from an old man he'd never seen before?

When the Cubs take the field the crowd doesn't exactly roar, it's more like a loud yawn. Every time I see these guys I wonder how they can be so bad. Man for man they look like the players on other teams, after an out the infielders whip the ball around the horn, the outfielders scratch themselves, the pitchers go through the same old routines before each pitch. But put these players all together and call them the Cubs and they turn into clowns.

I keep coming out to see them year after year because one year they're bound to break out or else nothing makes any sense.

While Pat Piper announced the lineups I started putting together one of my own: the worst Cubs I've ever seen. What about this catcher today? Moe Thacker. Name alone should qualify him. Of course he seems like a nice enough person. Whenever he puts on his uniform he goes rotten. Moe belongs.

Would the boy understand this lineup of mine? Here I've been taking him ten years. A decade of stinko baseball. Still he pulls for them to win! Back in the 30s, the 40s, this team had something. But now who'd expect anything but the worst? Dwight especially should know better. Understands baseball inside out. But here he sits, looking for a winner.

Two lines into the national anthem he says, "Francis Scott Key must have hated baseball."

From the way the old man tells me to pipe down, I can tell he secretly thinks I said something halfway funny.

Besides the American Flag, the team pennants, the Wrigley Field flag, they've got two others here. One, a big blue W on a white background. The other, a big white L on blue. At the end of every game they raise one or the other over the scoreboard. So people will know how the Cubs did today.

Mostly they see the L flag. The L from the el.

What with this Hi!Neighbor job of mine the old man and I didn't come out as often as usual this summer. Charlie and I came a couple of times but he doesn't care about baseball anymore, he only comes to shout stupid insults at the outfielders or try and get the beer man to believe he's old enough. He makes fun of the real old man, older than Hazard, who sits up near the catwalk talking to himself. "Passe from Passaic," he says sometimes, over and over. Who knows what he means? Worse than Hazard. Skid Row Joe, Charlie calls him. Mostly I don't say anything but sometimes I tell Charlie to can it. What business does he have calling this guy names? Just because the real old man doesn't smell so good wearing this big raggedy coat in the heat and drinking wine from a bottle in a bag (how does he get the bottle past the guard at the gate?), Charlie's got no reason to make fun of him. The real old man understands the whole game a hell of a lot better than Charlie does these days, and he causes no harm.

Where is the real old man today? He's always here by now. Passe from Passaic.

"It was a massacree," Hazard says. "A gory massacree."

Who knows? Another person I can't figure out. Hazard, Charlie, anybody. Charlie's the one who helped me out when Vince Balboni got me in a headlock. She must be a hooker, Vince said, and knocked the wind out of me with one punch. Cold day after school, cold and wet, I wouldn't tell Grampa how my pants got so muddy. In those days I didn't even know what hooker meant. What would Vince have done to me next if Charlie hadn't come by? But now Charlie's changed, now he's the kind who razzes an old man in a smelly coat. Shut up and watch the ballgame, I tell Charlie, and he tells me only a spaz would still care about baseball at our age.

I am a fool for caring about a bunch of characters standing around in suits that could double for pajamas while we sit here and wait and wait for something to happen. I know. But most of all I love the stretches of time when nothing seems to happen. Where else can you sit back and wait and watch, nobody telling you what to do? Grampa says you spend most of your life waiting but don't usually get to name the place where you wait.

Nobody else knows half what he knows about the game, half as clearly what the waiting is all about.

Hack, Freese, Crowe, Grimm. Jay. Derringer. Lynch. Lombardi. Heist.

Wait. Some of those are not here today. Some of those players are ex-Reds or ex-Cubs, gone, dead for all I can say. Names from the 30s. Saved out a penny or a nickel a day from piecemeal labor, came here once a month. Vera could have got in half price. She never wanted to come. The one time I asked. Spending a day with her here would not have felt any stranger than any other day of ours. Could I have showed a girl how Billy Herman turned the double-play best?

Herman to Hubbs. Thirty years of Cub second-basemen. At least I still know which played thirty years ago and which now. If nothing else I have passed this on to Dwight. The most useless knowledge of all. Anything else he will get on his own or not. If he turns out like me, not. I have nothing to teach him. The past was one type of pain, now another. Nobody teaches pain.

What just happened? Cincinnati. Homer by the Reds. Lynch? Lombardi? Wait. Lombardi's gone. Wait. Second inning already. Watch the game in front of you. Otherwise the kid will think his grandfather's ready for the glue works.

Tell him a tale. Let him know I know where I am.

After the shouting dies from Robinson's homer the old man coughs a couple of times, the quick cough he gives when he wants me to pay attention, and says, "Boy that one almost looked foul."

How does he know? Off wherever he goes when he stares at the ground he didn't see the ball fly out of here. He must be leading up to a story, most likely The Phantom Homer, The Great Darkness of '38, How The Cubs Stole A Pennant. Whatever he wants to call it this time.

"The umpire wanted home to his wife's cooking that day," he says.

"What day?"

"The Day of the Foul Homer. I was here. September Twenty-Eighth, Nineteen Thirty-Eight. Cubs came up in extra innings down by one. Score two and they'd win the pennant. Overcast day, getting toward dark when I stole a look at the scoreboard. Quarter to five, I had to leave. Pennant or no, I'd lose my job if I stayed longer. Night watchman then, a warehouse on Damen. Or Loomis, listen, forget the street.

"I got up. Only I couldn't make myself go down the nearest exit. Walked all the way around to left-field. Even then I wasn't the world's fastest walker. With the crowd here that day I had to extra-slow it. By the time I got to the other catwalk the Cubs had put a man on. Two out, new pitcher in for the Reds. Wait. The Reds are here today. Pirates maybe. Forget the team. Just picture me taking my last gander at the diamond from the left-field catwalk. Gabby Hartnett up. One last pitch, I told myself. Then I'll hit the road—"

Stopping short he gives some of his real coughs, they come from so deep each one must bring up a little of the mine. Then he stops coughing and takes away the rag from his mouth, drains his latest cup and sits there till I say, "What happened next?"

"Oh. That. One more was all she took. Hanging curve. Almost too dark to see, but Gabby took a whack. The thing must have had my name on it. He delivered it right to me on the catwalk. Last second a breeze got under the ball. Late afternoon breeze off the lake. Pulled it over my head onto Waveland Avenue. Otherwise I would be the owner of the ball that won the thirty-eight pennant."

He stops again, wraps his arms around his chest. Trying to figure out exactly how to tell the end, or trying to catch his breath. He never talks for so long at one time except to tell a tale.

"The umpire ran out to left, waving his hand to signal a homer. The Reds came screaming off the bench: Foul ball!

Screaming the ump must be blind. Meantime the Cubs hoisted Gabby on their shoulders. Carried him off. The pennant was theirs.

"Hell, that ump could not have seen if the ball went out fair or foul. Too dark. He wanted home to his supper was all. Wanted home so he called it a homer, no joke meant. Only one man knew. When the ball went over my head I was standing two steps to the foul side of the flagpole. I knew Gabby had not hit a homer. I wasn't telling. Who would have listened? Anyway, I had to get to work."

This little smile comes over him like he thinks he told it right for the first time, and maybe he did. At least he didn't go off on his usual trails leading to nowhere to try and recall one detail or another. Even though I know that homer didn't happen that way, he told it like he wanted me to believe him this time.

Does he think I forget I've told it before? A dozen times. Must drive him crazy. Make him want to leave more than ever. He wants to anyway. Not that he says anything. I know. Just like I know he only says "What in heck" when he's around me. Around his pals he must say "What in hell," or more.

Fine. Let him quit school, look for something better. Turn out a drifter like his father. Must run in the Cope blood. A drifter is not so awful. Long as you keep from getting tangled up with people. Whatever he does would be better than sticking with a half-dead old man.

Here we are, end of four innings, and the Cubs have regained the lead, as if they heard him tell the Gabby Hartnett story and took inspiration from a tale out of their golden age.

Halfway point. Now they stop bringing it around. Up here on the catwalk one man tries to handle this whole line. The thought of another beer must have given me strength. Not a moment of pain on the thirty-two steps up here. Only now it hits. Make that two High Lifes, buddy. High Lives.

The only park in America where everything happens in daylight. From the catwalk the light hanging over the field looks different than from down in the front row. Not as harsh. A golden light.

Or am I going nuts? Or is it the pain?

Before he counts my change I gulp down half the first. Straight into my lungs, dousing the pain. Beer man wonders why don't I step aside. Fine. Go lean against the fence. Look down on Sheffield Avenue. All told how many beers have I drunk at this windy spot forty feet above the street? Always gives me a dizzy surprise. Traffic down there. I forget life carries on during a ballgame. Even the wind I forget on a day hot as this. Until I come back up here.

The second doesn't douse the pain. The second leaves me with no place to go but the gents rooms.

The burning inside me. Let me out of this light.

Now comes the hour when the sweat runs down your face and the players move in slow motion or not at all. I keep waiting for a spider to come crawling out of the vine and go crawling back in after finding no sign of life here.

The Reds have a threat going, I don't even know how. I start picturing myself at a creaky desk by a window overlooking Malden Street some afternoon in January with Mister Butman droning on: The Commies want to take over this, take over that, the Commies hate the notion of a happy family.

Where did they find one to despise? I want to know, but figure if I ask he'll send me to Inside Suspension so I keep my mouth shut and sit there puzzling over what this Hygiene class is suppose to mean to a kid going nowhere in the world, or what it would mean if I was going somewhere, down a road, leaving the old man free, out of his hair. Eleven years is long enough for me to mooch off him.

But at least this year I'll have a spot on the *Bobcat*, which is a stupid name for a paper and which mostly prints letters complaining about the cafeteria and announcements by Doctor

Erie that he's got faith in all of us as the young leaders of tomorrow, but I couldn't pass up working for any paper where the managing editor is Judie ("That's how I spell it") Langerman. One day last spring the old man asked me was I sweet on anybody. At first I didn't know what the hell he was talking about, whoever says they're "sweet on" somebody? When I figured it out I changed the subject. Wanting Judie Langerman would have only been worth telling if I'd ever had the nerve to talk to her about something besides newspaper business. It was nothing to tell the old man.

But at least also no more Hygiene class, no more questions from Hazard: Are they telling you the whole truth? How am I supposed to know if they give us the whole truth when I'm in the middle of watching filmstrips of mother-father-daughter-son around the dinner table, breakfast table, picnic table, Christmas tree, so many shots of people smiling over their food I was ready to jump out the window. If they wanted to show us a happy family they should have sent us down to the Field Museum, to the displays of cave people, jungle people, fifty thousand years old. Whenever I stand by one of those frozen families I want to force my way through the glass and join them around their campfire. They're so ugly. They look so pleased to be right where they are, for good.

Where is the old man? Must be returning some of his beer to what he calls the great river of Wrigley Field. I wouldn't mind paying a visit myself but with this threat the Reds have going I'd better hang on.

We'd miss each other a little, at least I would miss his first-class grouching and these trips to the ballpark. But there should be some other place in the world where I can feel at home besides Wrigley Field.

The Reds send Lynch up to bat for Jay so the Cubs call in Spring with the bases jammed. What a name, Lynch, the most dangerous man around in this situation. On his card he looks like some gunslinger who hasn't bothered to shave for the last three days. How would it be, to be able to look that way just by not shaving?

The first pitch Lynch drives to deadaway center, going, boy is this one going, high into the bleachers, real gone, a pinch-hit grand-slam to give the Reds the lead again in this hopeless game. Now everybody's quiet except the ones laughing at how the Cubs can never hold a lead, and I'm wondering if the old man got out of the john in time to see the latest disaster.

Cool and damp. The damp stench. Eighteen gents around a giant tray, trying to lose the sins of the day.

How long has this pain been mine? Of too many beers passing out of me. Sharper than the one in my chest. Less familiar, sharper, funnier. Funnier, why? It comes out my privates, and is not about to kill me. There. There. There. Two dollars and some cents worth. Done. The pain fades in waves.

In the dark hallway it shot through me. Your daughter. That hot muggy day I drank more beer than today. The same pain a knife through my parts. While I read the wire.

Fine. The fire in my chest, but fine. Just let me lean. Rinse my face. Catch my

How did my face come to be so white.

And where did my face go.

And how in hell have I wound up on my knees. In my mouth black bits of the earth.

Somebody is blocking the door so I push harder, push my way in to where it's almost cool, and just inside the door a few men stand staring at the floor. Hazard crouches on his knees, bent over this little splotch of black blood, his mouth open with nothing coming out. For a few seconds I'm like the rest of them, all I can do is stare. Pretend this old man's a stranger on the floor of the dark almost cool Men's Room in the Wrigley Field bleachers. His face looks dead and white, his face makes me sick, the black mouth scares me. I want to walk right out. I walk past him to the sink. This man is nothing. This man is nobody. All I wanted is rinse off my face. In the mirror he is still down there. I turn the water on.

I turn the water off and go to him.

His eyes blink fast then and when his hand pushes me away I don't know what I'm suppose to do so I grab his damp cold hand and hang on. I bend down. His lips move until I hear, "I'm fine." You don't look so fine but he starts to his feet.

The other men go on about their business, all but this colored man. "You want an ambulance for your papa? There's a guard outside can get one right off."

Hazard shakes loose from my grip, he goes to the sink, he says into the mirror, "I'm not his pa." I turn back to that man and thank him anyway, "We don't need one it looks like."

Most everyone has gone back out. From the sound of the crowd the Cubs have a rally going. Hazard is splashing off his face. He's hearing the crowd too. When I follow him out my shoe almost sticks to the black spot.

"What the heck happened?"

What the heck, what the hell, what the more.

We stand by the fence over Sheffield. The breeze feels even better than before. Check the scoreboard. Two runs in. Check the bases. Two men on.

"Watch the game," I tell him. "Banks is up."

Ernie Banks. The one player on this team who can stand beside the guys I saw in the good years. No one would believe a man so skinny could hit the ball out of sight. We've seen him do it forty times.

This time I see every part of his swing. I see his hips turn as the weight shifts from one leg to the other. His arms whip the bat around, I see his wrists break. As if I can follow his eyes following the flight of the ball one second before he starts down the line. This flight needs no help from the

wind. This flight carries into Waveland Avenue. Across into a gangway.
The boy looks at me. He knows when he has seen greatness.

After a homer everything settles down. The crowd sits back. A few stay
on their feet shouting at the pitcher. Even though they know he can't hear
them. Tell him what a bum he is. This takes a while. The next batter steps
in. The boy asks another question.

"You want to go home now?"
"Walk out on the Cubs ahead in the eighth?"

So we tramp on back to our spots in the front row and for
once I'm the one who wants to take it slow. I still don't know
what happened back there. I want to get him home safe and
sound but if I said so would he follow my words?

By the time we sit down the Reds are up in the ninth for their
last chance, the Cubs are this close to a win, and then after the
first two Reds go down and the Cubs are that much closer
something funny happens. Pinson takes the first pitch, a beauty
on the outside corner, somebody behind us—probably the jerk
in the White Sox hat—shouts, "What do you want, Pinson,
eggs in your beer?", and now I don't care. Vada Pinson just
looked at strike one. So what? Sure, he has the power to tie this
game with a homer on the next pitch. What difference would it
make? What are we all doing here screaming at guys who can't
hear us, praying for someone to strike out, praying for a winner.

The next pitch Pinson lines a shot to right-center, deep and
rising, and I sit and watch Al Heist come charging back to stab
the ball on the warning track to end the game. Around us people
stretch, yawn, start to push their way out. They're in shock the
Cubs won a game.

Grampa says, "I want to sit here."

If it's up to me we can sit here for good.

After a while this popping sound comes from over in the
grandstands on the far side where after every game a bunch of
kids go running along the aisles pushing the seats up. Thwock!

you'll hear, then another Thwock! The place clears out. While their noise dies you can start to catch the breeze through the vines.

Who'd have thought the kid would walk in right then? Grab hold of my hand. Who'd have thought some stranger would take him for my son?

Pat Piper announces the totals. He has worked this job since aught-nine. What kind of life would that have been, half a century inside this ballpark? In the early days they didn't even have a public address system. Piper had to walk around the field, shouting the lineups through a megaphone. So the people would know. Shouting. His fool lungs out.

The sun has let itself down behind the upper deck, leaving the field in shadow, the outfield grass almost too dark to call green anymore.

"Aren't you going to see a doctor or something?"
"I know what I need to know."
"You do? What?"
Enough questions. What's he expect me to say, By crackie I reckon my lungs have pert near give out? He'll understand without my saying.

After four-thirty. We got to see a long game. Most of one. I saw one game that went longer than this. From behind we hear the pulling of ropes: Over the scoreboard, the unfamiliar flag. The huge W. A guard comes down the steps. Today I don't want anybody telling me I have to leave. So we get up and stretch. We start the long climb home.

△ △ △

Hobart, Arizona
Tuesday, October 9th
Dear Papa,

I'm safe and sound. Raymond and I arrived here yesterday in our new home. Just so you won't have to worry I can tell you I'm Mrs. Raymond Cope now. Please don't worry about me.

I'll write you again soon.

Love, Vera

2. City Room

Dwight comes running through the winter night, holding his side, hoping he doesn't look like some hoodlum just plugged by Richard Widmark. The eleven-block run often gives him this cramp in the side. When Dwight shoves a handful of dimes and pennies under the ticket window the man in the booth does not take off his sunglasses and look him over; after all these nights he seems to have decided the boy belongs here. Puffing quickly on his short black cigar the man pushes a damp ticket into the boy's fingers.

The Drake Theater opens at seven-thirty every morning. By the time Dwight shows up, many of the clientele have been here for more than sixteen hours. In return for their fifty cents they've enjoyed a whole day plus half a night of shelter, as well as five complete showings of a different double-feature from the one they sat through five times yesterday.

Most nights Dwight walks in during the opening credits or the first scene. On the best nights, this Tuesday turning to Wednesday in the middle of January for instance, he enters as the next-to-last movie ends, and gets a moment to settle into the darkness of the overheated house. Then he throws himself into the world of whatever movie comes on, the more improbable the better, and at the same time he holds back from that world to take in the theater itself and the few people in it and every once in a while remembers with a tightening in his chest that a few hours from now he will be back in school and a few hours after that on the el to work again.

The people he sees on screen enter his dreams, and there they are real. While he sits in the Drake they are at once real and unreal, strange and common, and his watching them is most strange of all.

Afterwards, walking up and down the long subway platform he notes every sound: the bald black man who claps out the Lord's praise; the wavering cry of a distant el, a rat scratching through the gravel beside the tracks. He can fall asleep standing up and still know the sounds.

Later he is slouched against a torn seat, trying not to hear the scream that rises every time the el finds a curve in the tunnel. In the middle of its passage between empty stations the el jerks to a stop while the overhead lights blink and blink and Dwight turns slowly to make sure he is alone. He likes having the car to himself. Every other car might be empty too, the CTA has sent out this train for him alone, or so he wants to believe. He closes his eyes, when he opens them he doesn't know how long they were closed. Has the el passed North and Clybourn yet, will the climb from underground into the Near North Side begin beyond the next long curve? Turning to peer for no good reason at the blank gray wall stretching beneath the city he is hit with his own reflection flashing bright and dim. The reflection frowns. His face must come from his father, the only resemblance to his mother seems to lie in a certain intent expression he thinks he can remember as hers, a look that comes to him when he sees himself in the el window wishing the ride home were over. His face has nothing in common with Cagney's, only a distant connection to Garfield's in the dark, sharp features.

This time when the lights flash off they stay off. Gently the train slows. Dwight closes his eyes to denser darkness, the train still moving very slowly, a steady rocking, and his mother's laugh is her own, steady and dry and quiet.

He sits up. He heard nothing. He heard his mother's laugh, her own and also the laugh of Veronica Lake in tonight's movie.

In the snapshot on Hazard's bureau his mother resembles Veronica Lake only slightly. The boy does not turn. Dry and quiet, the laugh of someone who knows something she isn't telling. He clenches his eyes shut, not knowing if he wants her to go or stay. Or if she is here or ever was.

Slowly the el enters the North & Clybourn station. The doors open for nobody. She's gone. She never came. He heard her. No, no laugh at all, only the slow rocking.

Walking down Lawrence Avenue under a slate sky he wonders if her feet touched these same spots in the brown and yellow snow, the rock salt. How much have the dark store windows changed in twenty years? Watching his own passage across each of these fronts he fails to notice a stretch of unsalted sidewalk. After his feet have slid out from under him and he has rested on the ice a few moments, the pain drifting through his thigh, he realizes he must have looked like a cartoon character for an instant, hanging in midair, awaiting his own fall.

At two-fifteen he lies in his bed. The laugh he heard or didn't hear, the cold walk from the el station, the definite pain in his thigh, these have awakened him. Now he has to lie a while in the frenzy of his night pictures before being taken by sleep. He wakes to the fierce breathing of his grandfather in the next room and to the clatter of a rare el in the last hour before dawn, wakes again to a garbage truck crunching through the alley snow. And he shivers through the retreat of darkness, and wonders if he can force himself to get out of bed and push the button before the alarm clock goes off. Lying on his side he watches dawn slowly illuminate the Great Scenes of American History displayed on the shade of the standup lamp, watches January light enter the faces, the bodies of the women on his walls, Carole Lombard, Ava Gardner, Gene Tierney; Rita Hayworth, very young, in *Only Angels Have Wings*; Bette Davis, Maureen O'Hara, Marlene Dietrich, Hedy Lamarr. Dwight hesitated a long time before taping Dietrich's picture to his wall. Of all the women, she alone looks straight at the camera, at him. He prefers pictures where the woman looks away, at something or someone else or at nothing. Where she seems to have something else on her mind.

Lying on his back he reaches for the cool touch of himself.

In the brown light of the kitchen he manages an hour of homework. From his grandfather's room come the muffled sounds of Hazard Harker getting ready for another day.

"How long you been up?" the old man asks, shuffling in.

Dwight says, "Half an hour, maybe," and Hazard answers: "Need more time than that for your schoolwork."

Dwight looks up at the clock over the refrigerator. "No, wait, I've been up a good hour."

Hazard answers: "You should get more sleep."

The old man dips a knife in his black coffee and pushes the heated edge into the butter. "It'll never get soft by itself in this kitchen."

Without looking up from his Chemistry book Dwight completes the thought: "Leastwise not in the dead of winter."

Finally Hazard says, "You coming in at two-thirty in the morning again tonight?"

Dwight takes the Drake schedule for January from his pocket and unfolds it with care. By this point in the month a strong tug could tear the schedule to pieces; by the end of the month it will be in pieces and Dwight will carry only the lower-right-hand corner.

"*Mildred Pierce*," he announces, and puts the schedule away. Having returned to his book he waits for his grandfather to say, "So?"

"I'll pass it up. I'm not much of a Joan Crawford fan."

When Hazard has finished the one piece of buttered toast, the half-cup of coffee, he says, "Ready for your test? I could quiz you from the book."

"I'll do all right." Then he looks up. The old man sits nodding and shivering, staring at the open Bible on his lap. The boy says, "You want a blanket for your shoulders?"

Hazard continues to nod. Lately Dwight has noticed him nodding more of the time. He wishes he were old enough to buy liquor and the old man could still drink. He'd make the nodding stop, bring home a fifth of rye and make his grandfather warm for good.

"I'm sixty-eight, not eighty-eight. When I want a blanket I'll get up and get one."

The boy has returned to his homework.

He studies his hands in the gray and green light of the schoolyard, too big for his body, the hands of a wide receiver. Admiring his hands, he almost forgets to run when the ball is snapped. His hesitation confuses Charlie Witt, who drifts over to cover another player, leaving Dwight free to cut an easy diagonal through the mud and wind up alone just in front of the end zone. To make the catch spectacular he leaps, hangs in the air for a fingertip reception before falling backwards across the goal line. From midfield his teammates perform a lethargic chorus of whistles and shouts.

Charlie jogs over, breathing hard. "Decent catch, asshole."

"Routine," Dwight wipes some of the mud from his pants and then drops the ball at Charlie's feet, spattering mud on the other's shoes.

"Don't be a jerk," Charlie says, and kicks the ball a long way off toward the street.

From back at midfield somebody shouts, "Nice play, Jose."

Charlie shouts back: "T.S., Mrs. Eliot."

He and Dwight slog to the fence where the football has lodged. On the street beyond, Vince Balboni is engaged in minute study of the innards of another greaser's engine.

—Heard your old man's a pimp.

What's a pimp?

—Heard your old man runs your mother's ass out at Sixty-Third and Cottage Grove.

They're gone.

—What do you mean, he's gone? Your mother croaked your father for peddling her ass?

And here Vince punched Dwight twice in the arm, and turned to his own grinning buddy.

—This guy doesn't know his old man pimps for a living.

He's gone.

—If he's gone then who peddles your old lady's ass?

Vince Balboni was the only other sixth-grade boy at Anson Elementary who was Dwight's own height, but he was stocky, his quick punches carried a sharp, confusing power. The worst of Dwight's anger came from knowing that he was about to cry.

Leave me alone, you never saw my mother.

—Then what does she do if she ain't down there on Cottage Grove? If you can't tell me it must be true.

Dwight threw up both hands and managed to push Vince's fist away, then the other fist crossed under Dwight's arms catching him in the stomach, knocking the wind out of him so fast he could barely feel himself crumple to the ground. Near the other end of the field three boys stopped tossing a football around and moved closer to watch.

—If you don't know what she does I could be right, right?

Vince knelt on Dwight's chest. In the midst of his tears the boy wanted most of all to shout at him to shut up, not because of his words, which Dwight still did not quite understand, but so his humiliation could at least take place in silence. Vince's buddy walked in quick circles around them, still grinning. Though Dwight couldn't breathe he found that his legs kept kicking up and out in a pointless struggle. Turning his head back and forth so he wouldn't have to look at Vince's face (and why was Vince so mad, why did he act as if Dwight had done him some wrong?) Dwight saw the heavy figure of Charlie Witt half-running through the mud. Vince wrapped Dwight's neck in the crook of his arm, shouting:

—Right? She's a hooker, right?

Vince's buddy walked in faster circles. Charlie ran up, slowly and halfheartedly as it seemed to Dwight, and said, Don't be a jerk, and picked Vince up by his belt and the back of his jacket, dropped him into the mud, picked him up again, punched him in the chest, and pushed him back into the mud. When even the release from Vince's weight didn't allow his own wind to return immediately, Dwight grew suddenly terrified and began to thrash around on his back, continuing to kick his legs up and out into the air. After Vince and his buddy had scrambled up and run off toward Montrose Avenue and Dwight's wind had returned he began to shout. While Charlie stared down at him he went on for a good half-minute, thrashing and bellowing, a display of rage and terror that even now, six years later, he can't recall without embarrassment.

"No fooling," Charlie is saying. "You've got the best pair of hands in this school. You should've gone out."

"I coulda been a contenda."

"Huh?"

"Forget it."

Dwight pulls the ball from the fence. Sure, he could have made the varsity, if he weighed fifty pounds more and lifted barbells and loved pain and didn't have a dying grandfather on his hands. Anyway, football season is long over. High school will be over soon. "It all stinks," he hears himself say, looking back at Vince Balboni bent over the car. Even on this sunless day Vince's hair shines.

In the sudden heat of Grimm High Dwight struggles to take a breath.

Hazard feels this way all the time.

What made him suddenly think how Hazard feels? He takes care of the old man; he doesn't have to worry about him, too.

"What do you say?" Charlie shouts. They are standing at their lockers, inside the din of young men kicking shut their lockers and young women slamming theirs.

"About what?"

"About what I just told you about, Cope! Me and Camille and you and this friend of hers, Friday night—no, don't tell me, your job—okay, Saturday night, the four of us—"

"Saturday night, sure! There's this great double-bill at the Drake—"

"Are you nuts? You don't go to the movies on a date like this. Especially not to that pit-hole."

"Where do we go?"

"My basement. My old lady goes out playing pinochle, all that stuff, so the place is ours."

"Uh-huh. Who's Camille's friend?"

"She doesn't go here. She goes to Saint Bernadette."

Dwight says, "Nobody gets anywhere with a Catholic girl."

Charlie's laughter carries around the corridor, which in fifteen seconds has become almost deserted. "What the hell do you know? You've got as much experience as the man in the moon, with Catholic girls or any other persuasion. Camille is Catholic herself, she just happens to go to Grimm. If something happens it happens, I don't care if the girl's a A-rab."

At the moment Dwight looks at the clock it jumps ahead one minute. "Well, my grandfather's got me on this curfew."

"What are you, a ten year-old? I don't know how you put up with that old fart."

"Me neither. Anyway, I've been looking forward to these movies."

Charlie whispers, but loudly, "Fuck your movies."

Instead of going to the Chem Lab Dwight finds himself

pushing open the door of the Boys Room. Four guys stand smoking and giggling by the radiator. "And then what did she say?"

They look at him for the moment it takes to realize he is not Mister Nebenzahl, the Boys' Advisor, also known as Mister Potato, making his early afternoon rounds. Dwight stands at the urinal, wishing he could shut out their chatter and stand here in peace. Nothing happens. He looks down, shifts his weight, goes back to staring at the yellow-gone-gray wall, and waits. How long can he go on using the excuse of the curfew? Since Dwight started into high school, the old man has never set a curfew for him. And where did he get such a notion about Catholic girls, and why did he think it worth repeating? He must have been desperate for a way out, anything not to end up alone with some strange girl on a couch in Charlie Witt's basement.

But then all girls are strange. He doesn't know a single one on closer terms than the loan of a pencil. He can't imagine any girl's hands on the back of his neck, around his waist. Not even Judie Langerman. Least of all her. The women on his bedroom walls are closer to him than any girl from Grimm, or from Saint Bernadette, could ever be.

He gives up and goes to wash his hands. The drain is clogged. Staring at the drift of scum across the water, a peaceful movement toward the edges of the sink, he smells his hands: meat loaf and mashed potatoes. This must be the smell of Brunhilde The Trayscraper's hands.

Maybe he's too young. Not even seventeen until June, while Charlie turned eighteen last month. What is he supposed to think of himself, anyway? Is he handsome, ugly, boring? Today he won't look in the mirror, he's had enough of those big tired eyes, his bony nose jutting out from the face of a starving man. How can this head and the scrawny body to which it's attached ever achieve a thing? Years ago he could believe the world might be his to make, and whenever he overheard teachers or other grownups refer to "kids today" he felt a fearful pride in his small body, pride at being still free of all the foolish errors adults carried around. His head, his body, were too young and smart ever to dream of making grownup mistakes. He would turn out a railroad engineer, cowboy, explorer, astronaut, baseball reporter, or, of course, baseball player, with infinite ease, and would leave the bonehead plays to others.

Now every day feels like a bonehead play. He has lost the delight of being a child, and held only to the fearful sense of being small. Without having gained any of the freedom of adulthood he has been locked into a dark and narrow world of work and of waiting for nothing he can name or imagine. Yes, his grandfather will die eventually; in the meantime, what will become of Dwight? That small and infinitely hopeful boy will move further and further away, leaving Dwight a small and tired man. Unless. Unless he finds someone to help him name whatever it is he is waiting for. Someone to pay that much attention.

The towel dispenser is empty. Reaching into the trash he hears one of the guys behind him say, "Jeez, what a spaz!" He rubs the damp towel around his hands until it disintegrates. He will be very late for Chemistry.

Even though the end of the school day means the start of work, he wishes it would come. The end will free him from wanting someone to look at him, and from the fear that someone will.

The night man in the morgue makes a proclamation on the evening of February first when Dwight comes down for the Groundhog Day file: "That Sheffield you work for's a pissant."

"What'd he do that was so terrible?"

The morgue man reminds Dwight of every pipsqueak who ever tried to pull a fast one in the next-to-last scene and got a gut full of lead for his pains. He is the only person on the Chicago *Patriot* who talks to Dwight.

"What'd he do? Nothing. The guy don't even drink no more. The word is"—the man likes to repeat this phrase, as if telling Dwight a secret—"the word is he used to drink with the best of them. I can buy that. I know a reformed when I see one. And now he talks to nobody. And look at the crapola he runs in the paper. Every year, a copy boy comes down on the night of February one for this file. Don't they get sick of running this junk? Not here. People expect crapola from this paper and el crapola's what they get."

Dwight nods. He has heard this tirade, he knows how awful the Chicago *Patriot* is. Yet to get this job he pestered the personnel office all of last September and October, showing up at least twice a week after school, hungry for an opening. He and his grandfather couldn't live off the old man's Social Security and what he himself made bagging groceries on weekends at the Hi!Neighbor. At least twice a week he came down to the personnel office, hungry for an opening, and when he didn't show up in person he called.

His own eagerness made him sick, but he had no choice.

At last this job came through. Working the evening shift meant giving up his spot on the staff of the *Bobcat*, which meant not seeing Judie Langerman nearly as often, but then since he could barely speak to her when he did see her the sacrifice seemed sort of minor.

On the day he was hired he was told, "This is a fine position for a young person starting out in the world, a position with a future." After three months on the job he still wonders what in the world these words were supposed to mean.

"Here." The morgue man hands him the file. "Take this to Mister Pissant."

Back in the city room Dwight overhears Joe Marino say to one of the reporters, "I've got to run down the Southwest Side.

Somebody opens their trashcan tonight and finds a lady's torso.
How do you like that?"

Dwight walks slowly to the tall windows at the east end of
the city room and, facing east and north on this moonless night,
he cannot find the lake. He knows that if he turned to the south
he would see all kinds of lights but he keeps his eyes fixed on the
huge area of lake that seems to be nothing but a giant hole
waiting to swallow the city, swallow Joe Marino, his cameras,
and the torso he is so anxious to shoot.

"Copy!" Sheffield calls. For the second time, the third?
Dwight runs over and Sheffield hands him a few typewritten
pages. "This Groundhog Day piece ranks right up there with
O'Donnell's worst. We'll run it as is."

While he walks the article to the semi-circular copy desk
where two silent old men sip muddy coffee from huge paper
cups, Dwight is wondering if the quality of the *Patriot* can be
blamed on the sense of humor of Arthur Sheffield. After
handing the piece to one of the two old men he stands near the
coatrack, where, hidden by overcoats, he can watch the night
editor at work.

Sheffield is one of the only men Dwight has ever seen who is
thinner than Dwight himself. He also stands several inches
taller, well over six feet tall, sits straight and gaunt at his desk.
Every night he wears a dark gray or dark blue suit, dark blue or
gray tie, and a look of containment, as if the discipline of not
drinking has meant giving up any expression, as if a simple show
of emotion will send him immediately back to one of the South
State Street bars that the morgue man claims he used to
frequent.

Studying the man Dwight tries to imagine how he could have
come to be night editor of the *Patriot*. Sheffield could not have
come from the same world as the other editors and reporters,
drab or constantly aggravated as they are. They seem exhausted
by too many deadlines, cigarettes, and cups of awful coffee,

Sheffield by the world. Nor would he belong in a Hollywood city room, where editors tend to weigh too much and smoke cigars while trying to bully their talkatively colorful reporters. This man leaves his cigarettes burning for thirty seconds while marking a piece of copy. Just when the cigarette seems about to go out he takes a small puff.

Why light up if not to enjoy your smoke?

Sheffield shifts in his chair and glances toward the coatrack. The boy steps out and walks away, back into his job. He goes on running copy, running for coffee, watching the clock, hitting the morgue for another file. And, as he does on nights when he wants to see the late show at the Drake, he approaches the editor's desk at eleven-fifteen to ask if he can leave twenty minutes early.

Sheffield looks up, his face blank, and nods. Dwight starts to ask another question, one he has wanted to ask many times, but Sheffield returns to the piece of copy in front of him. Eleven-sixteen.

Dwight goes to the east windows to see the huge empty place again. Surely the hole will swallow everyone in the city except himself, and every brick and street light. Every edifice but Wrigley Field, which will survive so he can go there alone, sit in a box seat down by the Cubs' dugout, look out at those hundreds of yards of grass and dirt. Wait, what about Hazard? Shouldn't the old man be spared? Maybe, if he agrees to drop this Bible business, the Jesus routine he has been on these past few weeks. As long as he still has the strength to come out to Wrigley Field he should be allowed to die in his own good time, sitting in the sunshine.

One other place will have to be spared, the place Dwight discovered after work one night last November, in his third week on the job. Instead of heading to the subway station after work that night he began walking south, across the bridge into the Loop, walking past stores that looked abandoned but had only been closed for six hours, office buildings where a guard without a face sat in the shadows by the elevator. Walking, past barrooms too dark for penetration even by sight, walking, he came upon the only place where a kid of sixteen could hope to be allowed to enter. He had never thought of the movies as anything more than a way to pass a winter Saturday afternoon. But tonight the Drake Theater was an alternative to home, to his own room. He knocked on the ticket window. After a while a man with sunglasses appeared.

"The last show started twenty minutes ago."

Dwight shrugged, and reached in his pocket for spare change. The man took off his sunglasses and stared at him and then told him to go on in for free. "Next time you'll have to pay, same as anyone else."

The boy sat on the aisle seat in the back row. Eight or ten old or middle-aged men sat in scattered spots. A couple of them slept, another mumbled and occasionally spoke phrases out loud. On screen a man and a woman were kissing. Dwight recognized Humphrey Bogart. Several weeks later he would see the woman in another movie and identify her as Gloria Grahame. For now he leaned forward, wider awake than he had felt in weeks. At first he watched the people on screen only as much as he watched the man who mumbled, but gradually he came to accept that the important people were up there in the light.

The next week he returned twice, both times arriving twenty minutes late. Then one night he asked permission from Sheffield to leave early.

"Why?"

Dwight hesitated, but only for a moment. "To go see the late show at the Drake Theater."

While Sheffield stared at him Dwight wondered if he could be fired merely for making such a request. Sheffield said nothing, only nodded.

By now the two of them perform almost every other night their routine of the request and the silent nod. Standing at the tall windows after receiving tonight's permission Dwight realizes the Drake, too, must be spared. There has to be a place where he can spend the hours between midnight and home.

Wrigley Field and the Drake, yes. Hazard, probably.

At eleven thirty-nine he puts on what used to be his grandfather's coat, for which he is almost tall enough but much too skinny, and rather than await the elevator he runs and leaps down the four flights of back stairs to the loading dock. Here he dodges around paper trucks, hoping to get honked at or sworn at by somebody, anybody, until finally out on the street he turns his face to the wind off the black river and darts across the bridge.

Taking the eleven blocks at his usual painful run he keeps hearing the morgue man's words about Arthur Sheffield and Groundhog Day, and while his own shadow overtakes him again and again he wonders if he will see it tomorrow in daylight or if winter will end very soon. Then he gives a hoarse shout of laughter at his own superstition.

Propped on the toilet tank, the face of John Garfield looks just past Dwight standing at the sink. The boy picks up the straight-edge razor and is wondering where to begin when his grandfather's face appears behind his in the mirror.

"What's there to shave?"

Dwight scrapes the razor gently through the soap on his cheek. "Shouldn't you be in bed, Hazard?"

"Don't call me Hazard. I'm sick of bed. If it's so late why shave?"

"I had to start sometime. Sunday night seemed right."

"You sure come up with some dandy ways of not doing your homework."

"I know, I'm so clever."

"Watch you don't nick yourself. Old razor."

The old man retreats to his bedroom. Through his bloody attempt at shaving Dwight can hear his grandfather turning the pages of his Bible, mumbling, coughing, can hear the whistling that is his breath. Nicking himself yet again he starts to swear, then sees the picture card of the Sermon on the Mount that Hazard taped to the bathroom wall today. Shaking his head in dismay he draws the razor along the same jawline, nicks himself again, does swear this time but silently, and again, silently.

Now he puts the razor down and stands staring at John Garfield as if the longer he looks the more chance there will be of the actor's features becoming his own. Then he picks up the razor and begins once more. When he thinks he must be finished he rinses off and in the mirror sees a boy's face full of red dots, red bubbles. Rinsing the razor of his blood he puts it away with the old man's brush and cup. He holds up the picture of Garfield beside the mirror. The resemblance is no closer.

He goes and puts the picture in the top drawer of his bureau. "I'm done."

"Hallelujah."

Dwight sits down to his homework, watched or not watched by the women on his walls.

When Linda Dierkes smiles and Dwight half-closes his eyes he can pretend to be reminded of Lauren Bacall. Linda's hair is not as long, her eyes not as large nor as heavy-lidded, her cheekbones not as prominent. Her mouth is smaller. But she moves her eyes in a similar way and her voice has a certain suggestive quality. When he hears Mister Gahagen call on her one day with a question about Andrew Jackson, he wishes she would answer, "He used to ride high in the saddle." Ever since seeing *The Big Sleep* a week ago he has pondered the precise significance of the dialogue in the restaurant between Bogart and Bacall. Nothing he can recall from Hygiene class last year explains their terminology. Three summers ago Charlie stole a book called *Dude Ranch Chambermaid* from a store on Broadway and one afternoon brought Dwight down to the Witts' basement and showed him certain passages that Dwight can remember by heart but that still do not quite make the dialogue between Bacall and Bogart comprehensible. Yet there the dialogue was, and here it still is in his mind many nights and days later.

After class he takes from his locker the fedora he bought at the junk shop last Saturday. Down one hall and then another, pushing along through the crowds he follows Linda. When she reaches her locker Dwight stops, puts the hat on, adjusts it, starts forward, stops suddenly, turns around, takes the hat off, clears his throat, puts the hat on again, and is still adjusting the hat when he strides up to Linda and says, "You want to go out to Arlington Park some time and watch the ponies?"

She looks at the hat, at the hands adjusting the hat. "What?"

"The horses. Bring along a pint and make an afternoon of it. Then pick up another pint and make an evening of it." His hands flop at his sides. "You know. Horses."

"Am I supposed to know you?"

"Not necessarily." His head has begun to itch. "We're in Gahagen's class." Right along the part, his scalp itches wildly. "But you know if you're not up for the ponies we could do something else, like for instance you might really go for this double-feature at the Drake—"

Crouching to put down his books, fumbling for the Drake schedule in his pocket, Dwight can hear Linda close her locker, click the lock, flip the dial for safety's sake. The edge of her skirt brushes his cheek. Staring after her he scratches his head while two immediate memories carry on a combat inside him: the warm rough sensation of her skirt against his face, and the absolute absence from her voice of the proper Lauren Bacall huskiness when she delivered her parting words: "I'm late for Home Ec."

With a calm surprising to himself he walks back through the now uncrowded halls to his own locker, hangs up the fedora, and in taking down his Algebra textbook pulls two more books down on his feet. Still calm, but just barely, he lifts the two books to the shelf, then he slams the books down and slams the locker shut and leans into it, pounding the door with both fists for he doesn't know how long until a hall guard comes up and stands beside him. At the moment he stops Dwight realizes how much his hands hurt. He glances at the hall guard: Mister Kemp, one of the more easygoing teachers. Dwight shakes his head in disappointment; he isn't even going to get in trouble.

Mister Kemp speaks in an almost friendly voice. "What seems to be the problem?"

Dwight stares at the locker: 1170, 1170, 1170.

"Young man?"

"Uh, I'm not sure."

"Aren't you feeling well?"

Dwight shakes his head.

"Then go see the nurse. This isn't Stillman's Gym."

After Mister Kemp walks away Dwight remains at his locker, hearing what he takes to be the echoes of the blows his fists made against number 1170.

Late in March comes a Friday night when the city does not freeze. Sheffield is sitting by the eastern windows of the employee cafeteria when Dwight wanders down for supper. Dwight takes a cup of coffee and a slice of stale apple pie and is about to sit at a small table near the kitchen door, where he can listen to the shouts and crashes from within, when he hears Sheffield call, "Copy!"

He looks up. The man raises his cup in greeting, and when Dwight comes over the man says, "You have to slouch in the corner where nobody can talk to you? Too classy for the rest of the clientele?"

Dwight sits down across from him, amazed to have heard so many words at one time, unsure if an answer is expected. Sheffield goes back to staring out the window. Standing by the cigarette machine are two janitors. The white man keeps pushing down on the coin return lever, without reward. Not seeming to mind, he keeps saying, "She what? She what?"

Yawning, the black man turns away. "No way I'm about to tell you." With what seems to Dwight an almost infinitely slow turning he bends to pick up his bucket and walks away.

Sheffield says, "It looks like the end of the world."

"What does?"

"The lake."

Sheffield is right: the lake is its old self again. The boy turns from that darkness, that great hole, to study the lined face of Arthur Sheffield, the slightly glassy eyes, tight mouth. The composure. He wants to ask his boss when he first saw the lake that way. He wants to ask him a lot of things. Carefully Dwight eats his pie.

Sheffield says, "The best thing is not to look out there at night. The best thing is to keep lying as long as you can."

Dwight burns his lips on the coffee. They sit in silence.

A waitress comes out and sits alone with a cup of tea at the corner table where Dwight usually sits. The boy watches the man watching her.

"Don't you think that's silly?" the man says. "When women streak their hair. Peroxide, or whatever she did."

Staring into her cup the woman pulls her tea bag out of the water and lets it sink again, and then again.

"My mother used to do that," Dwight says.

The image of his mother sitting at a mirror drawing a thin brush of dye through her light brown hair disappears. "But then her hair was already lighter than that woman's," he says, and then says, "She was killed in an accident."

"A long time ago?"

Dwight nods. He looks again at the waitress. "If she put on a few pounds she'd look like Brunhilde the Trayscraper."

"I beg your pardon?"

"It's like this. In Music Appreciation Mrs. Guest has been making us listen to parts of *The Ring*. And now every time I see this woman who buses the trays in the lunchroom I keep expecting her to start bellowing in German. She just looks like my idea of Brunhilde. When I tell Charlie Witt he says I'm out of my tree."

"He might be right," Sheffield says. "But I doubt it."

"Thanks."

"Don't mention it."

They sit in silence.

Dwight asks if he can ask a question. His face holding a faint smile, Sheffield neither nods nor shakes his head.

"How come you always let me leave early when you know it's for the movies?"

"Because I know. You told the truth the first time."

"But you said the important thing was to keep lying."

"To yourself. Not to other people."

When Sheffield returns his gaze to the window he is still smiling faintly.

"But I mean, well, this is a job. I get paid eight hours, why don't you make me work the full eight?"

"No offense, Cope, but the Chicago *Patriot* will hit the street on schedule with or without you. With or without me, for that matter."

"How could it come out without you?"

Sheffield almost laughs. His eyes hold life now. "Because a newspaper prints nothing. Anybody can edit nothing."

"But then why keep doing it?"

"Good question." His hands take a cigarette from his silver case. He puffs once, puts it down. "Because it passes half the night."

Suddenly he stands and swallows the rest of his coffee and takes one more puff before putting out the cigarette. "Time to get back."

"I'll be right up."

"Time for me to get back, not you. They give you half an hour for supper, right? Then take your goddamned half an hour."

By the time Dwight emerges into the kitchen the next morning Hazard has already finished reading the *Clarion*, and the two of them don't even get to fight over the sports section.

"Watch you don't get too much sleep at one time." The old man trudges out of the room.

Spring training has begun, the baseball season will come to life in a couple of weeks, but even though the air drifting in through the open window is the air for which he used to wait every March, Dwight doesn't want to read about baseball today. He doesn't know what he wants. Taking the front section he reads random lines, looks at pictures of world leaders, criminals, a homeless dog, and these pictures seem even more odd than the moving pictures of other strangers he watched last night. Arthur Sheffield edits nothing. Newspapers print it. Then Hazard spends a certain part of every day reading the nothing Sheffield edits. Even if he reads a different paper, all of it is the same. Dimly the boy can hear the old man tuning in a spring training game. He tosses the paper aside.

Walking down to Wilson Avenue he heads east, past Woolworth's, past mothers out shopping with babies in carts or in strollers or in their arms. He starts to call out hello to Tommy Rigney on the other side of Wilson. But Tommy would want Dwight to run across and pass the time. Although he hasn't talked to Tommy in months, he doesn't want to right now. Or is it because he hasn't talked to him in months?

Many years ago on any Saturday in spring or summer he could walk over to the Rigneys and there find a family: Tommy himself, his mother Patrice, his kid brother George, and almost always their young cousins Petey and Marie who visited on weekends from the Southwest Side where the planes coming into and taking off from Midway rattled every window in the house: or so the cousins claimed. In return Dwight claimed, no matter how hot a particular August day might get, that Arizona days were twenty degrees hotter. This claim the cousins refused to accept as anything more than silly bragging. Mornings were spent playing pinners on the front stoop or stickball against the Anson playground wall, games in which Marie played as well as Dwight and almost as well as her older brother Petey. Afternoons the threesome went to the beach, the ballgame, the movies, the zoo. Saturday nights while George said grace Dwight would keep his eyes half-open to see Patrice's gnarled fingers pressed together in prayer, to find out if Marie was paying attention to grace or giggling silently or trying to kick her brother under the table.

And one Saturday night in the hour between dessert and "Gunsmoke," during one of the hundreds of games of kick-the-can they played over the years, Marie came and hid with him under the back stairs. When he kissed her on the mouth (peach cobbler) she gave a small shriek. Petey came running to the mouth of the gangway and then ran back to the Dutch Elm on the front patch of grass, the Dutch Elm that Patrice said was dying, and kicked the can twice against the tree, once for his sister, once for the boy who had kissed her.

On the best weekends Patrice invited Dwight to stay over. He made the obligatory phone call, he heard Hazard say "Suit yourself," and all was well. He and Petey would stretch out on an array of sheets and comforters on the front room floor, whispering jokes deep into the night till at last Tommy announced from his bedroom: "Time to re-tire." Still Dwight lay awake, imagining Marie on a cot in her Aunt Patrice's room, asleep or not asleep.

The Dutch Elm did die. So did Patrice. Two years ago Petey graduated from high school and joined the navy. This coming June Marie will graduate from high school and get married. Dwight hasn't seen either in years. Watching people stand aside for Tommy as he moves down Wilson, he wonders what Tommy's memories of those Saturday nights sound like. Does he wish, too, that they could have gone on forever?

Marie's hair was an even deeper black than his own. Her mouth tasted of peach cobbler.

On a day this clear the lake comes into view from blocks and blocks away. He stands gazing at the shimmering sunlight as if needing to be convinced one more time that the lake exists. Three months from now he'll be out of school for good, spending day after day down there at the beach, at Wrigley Field, exploring these streets, free of school for good. He could call Charlie right now and the two of them could toss the ball around for the first time in 1963. The day holds just enough warmth to let them. And just enough chill to give them both sore arms tomorrow. He won't call. He wants to be left alone, or to know somebody he has never known.

But how should he go about finding that somebody?

The hell with it. Do something useful, find a birthday present for Hazard. Less than two weeks to go. Give the old man a real surprise this time, not another set of handkerchiefs or subscription to *Popular Mechanics* but something he'll remember. For as long as he has left. He would like something Biblical, but how can Dwight take seriously this newfound interest in such things? The little pictures of Jesus on the walls, the reading aloud to himself from the Gospels: where has this faith come from? Out of the blue. Out of knowing he's dying. The boy wants no part of this routine. He wishes he could give Hazard something to take his mind off that knowing, even if only for a few minutes at a time, a present that won't be devoured as part of the Jesus binge, but that might still give Hazard Harker a kind of comfort.

What chance does he have of finding such a gift on Wilson Avenue, on Paulina, Montrose, Broadway?

He turns around for home, turns back to the lake, turns again and breaks suddenly into a hard run for home, cutting down an alley into another, out on Paulina to the gangway and up the back stairs into the kitchen. He stops. Why did he run, why come back here at all? Who's here besides the old man?

In the living room he turns on the TV, leaves the sound down, sits on the floor gazing at two cartoon dogs chasing each other across the deck of a battleship. In the seventh grade Dwight realized he and Hazard were the only people around who didn't have a TV. The old man could go down to Smalley's and watch the Cubs games there, but Dwight had to wait for infrequent invitations from Charlie or for weekends at the Rigneys to watch the Cubs or anything else. One evening Hazard came home from work with a broken set. "Earl Simonson was ready to toss it, then he thought we might want it." It was the first set Earl and Shirley Simonson had ever owned, and it would never work as well as it once had, but that night Hazard played around with the insides and got some ghosts of Perry Como to appear, and then he took it down to a shop for the remainder of the repairs. Dwight spent that summer drinking Dad's Root Beer out of his grandfather's beer stein and watching inning after inning of every Cubs game he didn't see in person.

At first he learned a lot. He discovered quirks he had never been able to catch from the bleachers: the way Ernie Banks' fingers would move perpetually around the bat like the legs of a centipede; how some pitchers scowled at the hitters as if trying to scare them into striking out, while others looked perfectly calm, as if the game were their personal property. But by September he had actually seen enough. What did Hamm's Beer, Jack Brickhouse's endless chatter about almost anything, or the shots of fans waving at the camera have to do with baseball? Since that summer he has seldom watched the Cubs or anything else on TV. The set has remained on its front room stand, ignored except when the old man launches into a tirade against its existence.

Today, even with the sound turned down Dwight can feel himself slipping into a trance of boredom. Why get upset about not knowing anyone new, the nothing that newspapers print, or not saying Hi to Tommy? Why get upset about anything?

"I said turn that thing off," Hazard says from the bedroom. How does he know it's on? Relieved by the disturbance, Dwight obeys.

The old man lies paging through the sports section, beginning the day's second perusal. From the radio comes the sleepy buzz of Arizona baseball fans, but not the voice of Jack Quinlan. A year ago this week Quinlan, favorite Cubs announcer of both Dwight and the old man, was killed in a car crash not far from the Cubs' spring training site. Even today Dwight still half-expects to hear his voice return to the WGN airwaves. And if Quinlan's voice were to come back, then so might the voice of Vera Cope, of anyone who died in a car on an Arizona highway.

"You better get some schoolwork done today."

"I guess so."

Dwight takes the framed snapshot from the bureau, goes into his own room, and closes the door. He lies down slowly. Stretches out, slowly. The woman stands in the parking lot of a diner called Sammy's. Dwight can remember the place himself or has seen the picture so many times he thinks he remembers. Behind her lies an expanse of sand and cactus, light gray foothills, dark gray mountains. The woman's half-smile transfixes him. What could she have been thinking at this moment? Is the half-smile for Raymond Cope? And is there somewhere a picture of Raymond Cope that Hazard neglected to destroy?

Turning on his side he lets one hand slide across his mother. If only the too many women would be gone from his walls. He can barely call forth a face to match the face in the snapshot. Only her laugh remains, and when he closes his eyes the strong smoke of her cigarettes, the coffee on her breath and lipstick around its edges. Her steam iron hissing in the cooler evening, pressing his father's shirts. Dwight came up and stood beside her, face buried in her housedress. The coarse feel of her dress against his skin, the soapy smell of herself: in remembering that smell he holds her in himself. If only he still knew the smell of those shirts she ironed. Her lips touched his forehead before she went back to pressing his father's shirts in the desert evening.

One night he woke crying from himself running after another dark-haired boy across the floor of the desert, burning his feet as he ran, the other boy moving further and further, Dwight's feet on fire. Coming to him she told him he could sleep in her bed. Our bed she called it. But when he went in and climbed under her sheet she didn't get in with him but sat at a table by the mirror. Still he couldn't sleep, not because of his nightmare but from wanting to watch the curve of her arm drawing the dye brush through her hair, to study in the mirror the front of her nightgown, the dull flash of her fingernails, and her face, frowning when she leaned forward to watch her own movements more closely.

Lying there he thought he could stay awake forever.

His mother is no longer a memory now but with him in this room, herself. He keeps his eyes closed. Her presence frightens him. This was her room. She lay once in this bed, a thousand, three thousand times. If he keeps his eyes shut, doesn't turn around, satisfies himself with the scent of her breath and her cool hand on the back of his neck, can he ask one question? Why did his father desert them? And then can he ask why she had to go and have her accident and leave him behind? But that would be two questions.

He can ask away, but won't get one answer. She's leaving. Why did she return for those few moments to his self-made darkness?

But that would be a third question.

The voice of Nat King Cole comes into his head, the opening song on the soundtrack of the movie he saw last night. In the slow sureness of the man's voice Dwight loses himself. "I'd rather have the blues . . . than what I got right now."

Somewhere nearby a man is going on and on about Abraham Lincoln. Dwight's gaze is held by the cars passing beneath the classroom. Why don't these people have to be at work or in school? Some of them are housewives out shopping, but the men, are they door-to-door salesmen? Hired killers? And the boys: greasers? car thieves? Or do all these people work evening shifts somewhere, like Dwight, and spend their days driving aimlessly through the North Side? The aimless turning of wheels. A car passing silently down narrow streets. Adrift.

When his chin drops forward he wakes to the sound of choked laughter.

"Are you with us, Cope?" Mister Gahagen says.

Dwight rubs his eyes. "You bet."

"Then how about telling us a little something about the Thirteenth Amendment, if it wouldn't be too much trouble."

"The abolition of slavery," Dwight says. "First Lincoln handed down the Emancipation Proclamation, July first, eighteen sixty-three, and then after the Union won the Civil

War the Thirteenth Amendment was ratified but not till after Lincoln was shot, which happened on April fourteenth, sixty-five."

"Maybe you should teach this stuff, Cope. You're probably smart enough. But then you'd have to stay awake, and that would be asking too much of you, wouldn't it."

Dwight sits there, not sure if he is serious. "Wouldn't it?" he says again.

"Well, no, Mister Gahagen, I should be able to stay awake."

"Well, Mister Cope, aren't we the lucky ones?"

"I do have a question, though," Dwight says. "You know the scene in *Young Mister Lincoln* where Henry Fonda is defending the two brothers accused of murder and he uses the almanac to prove they couldn't have been seen at the place where the murder happened because the moon wasn't out that night? What I'm wondering is—"

"Scram. I'm sick of you."

Dwight gets up slowly, again unsure if the teacher means it. "Where should I go?"

"Out in the hall. Stand there. Don't read, just stand. Right now. And if somebody asks, say you're doing time for sleeping in class."

The sneeze explodes as Dwight is reaching for the doorknob. It shakes him so hard he drops his books. He takes a huge white handkerchief from his pocket and while trying to gather his books he tries also to blow his nose.

"Look at the snotrag," shouts a boy. "This kid's a queer!"

Gahagen points. "Owens, don't be a smartass!"

After he has gone out and closed the door behind him he can hear the others howling at Gahagen's final word. Then he can hear his own heartbeat. He wishes Gahagen were dead, not because of this discipline but because he is a drudge, they're all drudges, every teacher he has known in this school. So are the students. Probably not one would make the connection between the Lincoln played by Henry Fonda and the one Gahagen has been talking about. Nor would any of them recognize the trademark of Victor Mature as Doc Holliday in *My Darling Clementine*. Does Linda Dierkes think he's a queer because of his white handkerchief? Dwight couldn't care less. He made his attempt with her, and found out she wasn't worth the trouble.

In a few weeks he will receive, in return for his four years here, a worthless diploma, and not the slightest idea where to go next. A lot of the others will go on to college, most to Champaign-Urbana, Jerry Garth and a couple of others to Yale, Stanford, names on the book covers sold at the school-supply store to jerks like Dwight. A few, Charlie for instance, will head into the service. Some of the girls will start having babies. Who knows, maybe Linda will have a whole household of little screaming Lauren Bacalls by the time she hits twenty-five.

Where will somebody like Vince Balboni end up?

And somebody like Dwight?

He hates feeling sorry for himself more than anything, except maybe when a happy ending comes along out of nowhere to ruin, or almost ruin, a good movie. He has no choice. He can't help feeling sorry for the sound his own heart keeps making in this bare corridor, where the only other sound is the droning of all the drudges behind all their doors.

The old man stands in Dwight's doorway, watching the boy put on his shoes. "Sunday nights now, too? You'll lose your mind with these movies of yours. Then where will we be?"

"I don't know," Dwight says. "Where are we now?"

"I'll tell you where. I'm praying to Jesus for three more months of life to see you graduate high school. You're doing your damndest to flunk out."

Dwight laughs. "I couldn't flunk out of Grimm if I tried. And why would Jesus care if I did? Anyway, tonight is *Lost Weekend.* Ray Milland."

"Lost weekend is right. You don't even do your schoolwork on Sundays anymore. Just lie around like some lounge lizard, blaspheming every chance you get."

"I wish I had back every weekend I ever wasted on homework."

He puts on his gray windbreaker, another piece of clothing that still bears the smell of his grandfather. Hazard follows him to the door.

"Why do you hide your light under a bushel? A boy with your smarts could have done well in school. Double-promoted out of first grade and then downhill all the way. Other boys have had outside jobs and still finished at the head of their class."

"I'll graduate. That's enough."

"Enough for you. Imagination of a lounge lizard."

As soon as he sees the window of the junk shop he realizes he will have to ditch school tomorrow afternoon so he can be back down here the minute the shop opens. The statue in the window, its flashing light a beacon to all passersby (but Dwight is the only passerby, the only one walking toward the Drake at 7:10 this Sunday evening): it is meant for Hazard alone. Did the owner of the shop leave the light flashing all Sunday so Dwight would see it?

The owner knows him, if at all, only as the silent boy who buys photographs of actresses, who bought, recently, one of John Garfield. A coincidence, then, a perfect one.

Lost Weekend starts in three minutes. Dwight hurries on. He'll return tomorrow, one o'clock sharp, he will ditch Chemistry for this.

Through the mild night, as alone as Ray Milland before the happy ending, Dwight walks. Ray Milland is Sheffield, trying to hold out against the bottle. But Ray Milland is watched by nobody, like Dwight. Ray Milland would not be there if Dwight didn't see him. Who is more important, the actor or the ones who let him stand in the light? When the movie ends the watchers go their own ways back to rooms where they live like the man played by Ray Milland, like Sheffield, trapped in a small room. Dwight lives alone, talks to a half-dead man in the other room who tells him he has no ambition, goes to school among strangers. He sits in an almost empty theater looking at strangers, goes to work where he watches a man who lives alone in a room, like the people in the Drake, like Hazard. His mother lived alone because his father came and went and then went for good, and then Hazard destroyed every picture of Dwight's father and cut him out of every picture he was in with Dwight's mother so that the boy not only can't remember a face but has no picture to help him bring back a presence. For all he knows his father might be alone this moment and all this night. Hazard and Dwight have the picture of Dwight's mother to remember her by, and they are alone. Even when Hazard pretends to have Jesus for comfort he is alone. Dwight's mother was watched by no one but Dwight. Dwight walks down a street that for these few moments is empty of a single car or the sound of the Loop el. He stops. Not even a voice from *The Lost Weekend*, not even his mother's laugh. Only shadows, and these are few and not real, not random, but placed as if in the set of a city held by the silence of night, carefully placed for the thrill of aloneness. If only he could tell someone the story of Ray Milland, lost like his mother, not saved in a happy ending, lost, gone, for good.

In bed he hears the wind off the lake, the breathing of Hazard. Would counting the ticks of the alarm clock put him to sleep? Or maybe if he speaks out loud to the man in there who seems almost never to sleep anymore, his words might put both of them to sleep. He clears his throat, lies tense, waiting for himself.

"Hazard?"

Same breathing. Same wind. Then the rough surprised voice. "You call?"

"I saw this movie tonight."

The old man doesn't answer.

"This guy, he's a writer, or he wants to be. You know Ray Milland?"

He doesn't wait for an answer, he knows the old man never went to the movies before he got too sick to go anywhere.

"He stays in his room, trying to hold out, wanting to write. There's a woman who loves him, but he can't make himself stop drinking not even for her. Not even for his writing. Even when he knows his drinking will make him alone forever. That's the movie. This man, alone. He ends up pawning his typewriter for another bottle. He ends up just about going crazy."

The same wind. But the breathing comes easier now. Or so the boy wants to believe.

△ △ △

Sunday

Dear Papa,

We've been here almost a whole week but the days run together when the sky stays the same blue.

So many times this week I've started to write and then torn them up. Even now I'm not sure what to say. You raised me from a little girl and sometimes I get scared to realize I've left you behind.

I wish after we settle down here you could be a guest. Does this sound strange? You would find things in common with Raymond, he knew hard times the same as us, the same as you. Not exactly the same, but hard.

Don't go thinking he tricked or forced me into this, he was the one who kept telling me to think over my decision before rushing into a move I might later regret. He wants to settle down and rest, he's told me so many times he's tired of drifting.

I want to tell you how we live. Right now we're staying in a couple small rooms over the garage. You'll like this, the morning after we got here he went down and started working right off. Leo, Raymond's boss who owns the garage lived in these rooms for a while when he got back from overseas but now he's bought a new house on one of these tracts at the edge of town. After being here for some time so we can get help from the bank we plan on buying one ourselves. Also Leo might make Raymond co-partner. Meantime I've tried to make this place feel like home, which takes some doing since after all a single man lived here.

Ray says I should send regrets for the Cubs losing the World Series.

Our address: Comanche Road, Hobart, Arizona. A lot of places have Indian names though I still haven't seen one yet. Be sure to write C/O Leo Whalen, this is assuming you do write back, which you know I hope you will soon.

Take care of yourself.

Love, Vera, your daughter

Pa,

Thanksgiving feels strange when the temp gets up to 94. It feels wrong. Sometimes I get a look at a Phoenix paper and check the weather in Chicago wondering if you're watching out for yourself and hoping the winter goes easy on your lungs. With the war over you ought to switch back to days, then you won't have to wait for the bus at dawn.

But I have good news now which you can probably guess. He or she's due in mid-July. Thanksgiving seems like the right time to tell you though like I said this one has been hotter than I knew it could be.

Marv and Lucille had us over for the day, also Leo came. Marv owns half the garage or slightly more, I don't quite get it since I thought Leo was sole owner or so he told Ray. Through most of dinner Raymond and Leo swapped stories. Asthma kept Marv out of the war so he spent these years doing something called Developing Properties and running the garage. As opposed to Leo who likes to tell a tale Marv mostly sits smiling this little smile like he's ready to spring a surprise. They live over in Centinela so I can't visit Lucille since Ray still hasn't gotten around to teaching me to drive and it's twenty miles. Maybe it's best, otherwise I'd be going over there and bothering her all the time. Josie seems nice too though kind of a loudmouth for four. Lucille's giving me all kinds of tips to help me through the next months.

Did the Rigneys have you over? Give my best wishes to Tommy, will you do that for me please?

Vera

Dear Papa,

Instead of a fancy card I'm just sending this note so you'll know I'm thinking of you. Wish I could send you a present but finding one for you never was easy and since you didn't write back after I told you the news I don't know if you'd like anything I could think to give you.

Hope this got (gets) to you by Christmas.

Love, Vera

3. Night Road

And so he asked me and when we kissed the second time after I said yes I saw a desert. When we kissed the first time after I said yes I shut my eyes and saw our escape route out of Chicago but not this long knife through flat fields but a twisting mountain road. Did I think mountains grew up out of nowhere the minute you left Chicago? I kept remembering Ann Sheridan and Humphrey Bogart on the run on a road through mountains. We're not running from the law but when we cross the border I tell Ray I want to get out and touch Missouri ground. Ray's dark eyes go black, a laugh lighting up his whole face like I'm a little crazy, but I remind him I haven't been out of Illinois since before I can remember, but Ray, he just drives on.

I know the ground feels no different this side of the line. I wish we would've stopped anyway.

Not Ann Sheridan. What's her name? Ida Lupino. I thought we'd find mountains but now we're here on a road different than I thought and I don't want to miss a thing so I'm staying awake till my eyes hurt and I start to see things. Watching the clouds all of a sudden they start to look friendly, who knows why. Night clouds over an open field shot through with moonlight is something I never saw in Chicago.

And when we kissed the second time I shut my eyes again and saw a desert.

"Maybe some coffee," he says. Against my face I feel a light from a sign—EATS—hanging over a roadside diner. An old man coming out holds the door for me till Ray comes up and grabs hold of the door himself. The man's hair is gray and wiry but this man is older than Hazard, smaller, smiling he tips his hat to me before stepping slow down the wooden stairs. Ray watches that old man get in a car even older than ours and start off down his own night road. He can't stand another man even tipping his hat to me. Ray's dark eyes. He makes me feel we're already married and he thinks a husband is supposed to act this way. I tug at his sleeve. He makes me smile when he gets like this.

Dark, still dark, he couldn't be home yet, has not read it yet.

We're not already married. Some time tomorrow, no, now it's today, we'll stop and let a Justice change us over. Then we'll find a hotel. Husband and wife. I can't picture the room, a bed for two, the light coming in on the bed or night falling. Last night sitting down at my cracked wooden table I tried to write a note and shutting my eyes I couldn't see our room then either, could not imagine where Raymond and I would end up.

"Dear Papa." Might have been the last evening of Indian Summer. Why did I say Papa when I call him Hazard to myself? "The light through my window seeps into the gangway, there's a pigeon on the ledge watching me. Don't worry please I will always be your daughter." Did I write those words to make him think I will always hate him? He'll hate me, blame me, and I'm sick of us pushing blame on each other. Our life was not his fault, the home he tried to make, days when the radiator never came on. Or the rules he set down, home by a certain time, not his fault for making those rules or mine for breaking them. If I hadn't I'd have never met Raymond, would not be here looking at these tall trees across the road from the diner scaring me for no good reason, since when are trees supposed to be scary? You'll end up crazy, Hazard would say, but not his fault. I'm tired of blame.

One night he came home with a radio and asked me could I

beat the dumbness of people throwing a radio out just because it broke down. Right there in the living room he worked on it, let me plug it in, and time after time we got nothing but a long deep silence. After each swear word he told me one or two were okay for him but I shouldn't assume I had free license, nobody wanted to hear a girl my age cuss.

The sixth or seventh time I plugged it in, out of that silence came a trombone playing a slow tune I had never heard. We couldn't make the radio go very loud but those low drawn-out notes filled the front room. Some summer nights when I couldn't get to sleep I'd take a pillow and lie out on the couch and turn the radio on. Every time you moved a muscle that couch's springs dug into your bones but I had the late night music and dibs on any breeze that found its way in from Paulina. Even with a car going by, or sirens, or a drunk shouting back at somebody shouting down at him to stop singing in the middle of the street in the middle of the night the front room still felt more restful than my own little den where the heat itself seemed to come wide awake in the summer dark.

My room only felt okay in the daytime and then only if some light snuck in to make them shine, my things, the rocks and bits of glass from the beach. Every time I went there with Thelma and Flo and sometimes Tommy and Lou I'd bring something home. Along one wall I set up a row of cardboard boxes and put out my things on display like I lived in a storefront on Michigan Avenue, except no storefront ever had such wild hunks of finery as my room. Hazard used to stop in my doorway, look at them all, and never say a word. He must have wondered why I put pennies on display, pennies I found every March when the snow melted. Why didn't I spend them on candy or fruit?

He never knew I stole. I'd look at those pennies and think, I don't need you, I can get an orange or pear whenever I feel hungry and you'll be sitting right here when I come back.

We should get food here, not just coffee, we don't just want to keep ourselves awake but alive too, Raymond and me, but no, I didn't steal whenever I felt hungry. Just once in a while. Not long after mama died I started, when we didn't know things would ever get better, didn't know we were caught in the worst time of all and maybe we weren't, who knows if a Depression is the lowest you can sink or war is lower? I could ask Ray right now, Is war the worst you can live through, you know better than I ever could. I don't ask him a thing. The war's what he never wants to talk about. "I used to steal," I say, standing at the diner counter, and Ray, he looks at me such a long time I get afraid he doesn't know me and then when he smiles it goes right through me like he means to smile at something out on the black road out there. So I tell him no more. Tell it to myself.

One Saturday morning just walking along Wilson trying to not think about feeling hungry and to figure out where I could go this early—too cold for the beach, too early to find Thelma and Flo and sneak in the Granville—going by McMichael's Produce I saw a box of oranges right out there, nobody around not even that tall crosseyed boy who used to stand guard waiting for McMichael to break down and give him a penny or a handful of peanuts. Instead of slowing down I walked faster, turned on Wolcott and walked faster past the bakery. By the alley sat Walter the fat shoemaker in a sagging wooden chair, he stared at me till I had to stick my tongue out at him to convince myself he didn't know what idea flew around and around inside my head. Cutting down the alley I made it back to Wilson where I could see the stand was still deserted.

Again I didn't slow down, my hand reached faster than I knew it could to take hold of an orange and pull. I only started running when I heard the rest of those oranges start tumbling out of the box into the street.

So I stole now and then, from McMichael's, from Cuyler's candy store. I could say I stole those pennies from the melting snow or the stones from the beach, I could say Hazard stole the radio from the junk man, but I know the difference: The pennies were lost, the radio had been thrown out, but the fruit still belonged to somebody. I didn't care, that's what was wrong with me, I couldn't care less that somebody else still owned the fruit. My hunger mattered more. Later on when we had a little more to eat the stealing stopped. I went on saving the pennies I found, I liked to look at them and know I didn't need

This kiss this kiss must be the lips of Raymond Cope it tastes of coffee. But I never object how he tastes, coffee, whiskey, cigarettes. He turns away and starts the car, we're pulling out of this place and only now the things I just saw inside come to me like the run in the back of the waitress' stocking when she turned to pour our coffee or the little girl and her kid brother studying the candy bars in the glass case. The boy, he might have been an Indian, who scrubbed pots and pans, steam coming up into his mouth. These sights have moved into my past now like the feel of the kiss Ray just gave me, like the kisses we shared at the lake last week. I wanted this night to be different. To see every single thing as it happened but now the night passes without my knowing each sight gone too soon. A tree alone by the road as we drive slowly by slowly picking up speed, dark shapes beyond, bushes pointing in many directions against the night sky that has grown white. Gone into my past, Ray's hand starting the car, the first taste of this coffee. Before I can tell if these shapes are friendly, gone, the young man in khaki trousers who sat alone eating pork chops and hash browns. He didn't know someone watched him wondering how he could eat pork chops this time of night. He is gone into my second sight. And Hazard would say if I keep thinking these thoughts I'll end up gone too, gone crazy and maybe he'd be right.

But then every second thing I did or said made him call me that or drove him crazy himself. The slapping sound my house slippers made on the kitchen floor when I'd go in to fix breakfast, this one sound he claimed woke him from his last half-hour of sleep and a person with one ounce of consideration would walk barefoot in dead of winter. Some mornings he's up first and then I get to hear him shave, muttering, grunting, humming, cursing when he cuts himself. Some mornings the sounds alone were enough to tell me I'd go completely insane if I had to lie there one minute longer. Those mornings I'd get up and stand in the bathroom doorway watching him shave. If I didn't have to only hear him, if I could see him at the same time for some reason that made me believe I might stay not-crazy a little longer.

Then we sat in the kitchen downing our usual breakfast, coffee and toast and cereal, Puffed Wheat Sparkies for me, oatmeal for the old man, and when we eat eggs and bacon he says I still hold my fork like a girl and when will I grow up. Icicles hung from the telephone wires above the vacant lot between us and the tracks where the el clattered by in the morning dark. One morning he asked me was I going to play hookey again today but I just studied the icicles till he asked again. I don't feel like going to some school where the teachers treat me like a dummy and the other kids make fun of my ratty clothes I say and then he started yelling I could goddamn well get out and find a job then, never saying what job he expected a girl of fourteen to find when he had to make do with piecemeal labor. I didn't argue. I despised our fights. Even after he got over hitting me when he got mad I still hated our fights most of all. That morning I decided to see what going to school every day was like.

Grimm High gone into my past like Ray's lips on mine before he started the car. These rows of corn, a pile of white stones by the roadway, gone already. Slow down, Private Cope, not for careful sake but mine.

I started reading everything I could find, newspapers, his father's Bible, cereal boxes, movie magazines. Even the textbooks with GRIMM HIGH stamped in purple letters along the side and the names of a half-dozen kids who'd had this book before me written inside the front cover. I found Tommy's name in my History of America book and in some of the margins in the same writing, "Who cares?" or "Big deal" or "So what?". My own name went right below his. Vera Alice Harker. I wanted to cross out the Vera. Who was Vera Harker to me, some woman who died long before I knew her after spending most of her life raising her sons and not doing much of a job of it to judge by the one I've had to live with. I wanted Alice, ma's name to be mine like her eyes in the picture in my suitcase now with me, with us. But in all my books I wrote Vera Alice Harker for fear of Hazard's anger if he found his mother's name gone and to remind me I was his daughter all those times I wanted to forget.

Spring nights I stretched out on the couch and turned on the radio and the standup lamp and lay there gorging myself on those books till Hazard called out from his bedroom to shut everything off or we'd go broke on electricity and he'd lose his job for lack of sleep. By that spring he had steady work in a defense plant out on the West Side. He'd stopped ranting and raving about how the government played into the hands of the rich and then tried to placate the Reds by offering handouts to the poor. Now that we're fighting a war we've got no choice but loyalty. He went and bought a lampshade showing Washington crossing the Delaware, Lincoln freeing the slaves, some pilgrim trading beads with an Indian, and the other Roosevelt charging up San Juan Hill. Since I was reading about America now I could do it by the light of her great men.

Even my reading drove him crazy. Now that I liked school he thought there must be something wrong with it. Before turning in for the night he would stand in the front room doorway pretending to have other things on his mind, humming along with some tune and sometimes just staring at me in wonderment. I didn't understand that look then. All I knew was I wished he'd leave me alone. Now I wish the old Vera could have stayed behind to be there when he reads my note while this one, me, moves farther and farther from him. The other one can stay and make him see how some of this was his doing, how he shouldn't have taken high school from me, should not have robbed me of that one thing. The war wouldn't have been lost. He made me feel it would be. My sophomore year he started in, next fall you'll turn seventeen that's old enough to come work in the plant because where's high school getting you? A girl doesn't need an education especially not one as pretty as you.

Look at me Raymond, tell me what kind of face you see in your eyes like the heads of nails.

Me and pa we both know I'm not pretty, hair the color of Post Toasties and the kind of face people call interesting with pa's wide mouth and long slightly crooked nose and the same pale close-together eyes that look out from the picture of ma that used to sit on my bureau and rides along now in my suitcase in the trunk of this Model A. I'm no beauty. Pa said it anyway and went on saying I didn't need school because in wartime people give up what they don't need like Tommy Rigney quitting school and signing up the day he turned old enough.

I didn't have the heart to point out Tommy quit right about the time they got ready to expel him for only showing up when he felt like it.

Tommy's hand on my face, my forehead.

But I'm here now.

The light falling into the gangway, the pigeon on the ledge. Ray's hands on my legs but he stopped.

But he's here now, him and me in this '39 Model A, farther and farther. The man beside me proves I'm here or else when he looks in this direction he'd see nothing, he makes me *her*, the *you* to his *I*. Otherwise he would not see a thing or else why drive this road through the dark?

For a while he gave up trying to talk me into it. For a while he used the silent treatment. I come home from grocery shopping and start to explain how I portioned out the reds and the blues this time and he walks out of the kitchen and goes to turn on the Lone Ranger or Terry and the Pirates. After supper, using some Old Dutch on the stains that never magically disappeared I'd tell him something that happened in school, take the rally we had in the gym for War Stamps and as soon as I get to the best part when Lou de Maestri set off a smoke bomb in the middle of Colonel Jansen's speech from the OCD pa picks up the paper and rattles the paper and makes believe he has to mumble every word. Till I gave up my story and went back to sloshing that half-lukewarm water over our plates. I didn't mind fixing breakfast or supper or washing up after except when he wouldn't talk or let me talk. And then a week went by where we don't say one word.

In the silences I wondered was he right. But I actually liked sitting in the yellow rooms with high ceilings listening to the radiator bang and hiss and watching the teacher's hand move across the board leaving a white trail of words or geometric curves. Mrs. Gerwig had blue hair and wore the same stale perfume every day. Once she took me aside and asked me why was I taking Latin if I wasn't in the college-prep group. To me it was a chance to see and hear something different from what I saw and heard everywhere else every day, the long lists of odd words I tried hard to memorize with their endings changing on you for no apparent reason. Either she didn't understand my answer or she was going senile but every few weeks she asked me again but still always let me stay in the class even if I didn't do such fine work. Maybe she felt grateful. Few enough of us wanted to hear her old dead language. Her words became this mysterious part of my day, *tabula, cupio, mentis*, like her perfume and the little smile she wore no matter what the other kids whispered right in front of her cold eyes.

Tonight. This night. *Hic nox*, driving past another farm, *agra*-something. *Via longa* past many *agras* and even more *arbor*— but what would be the right ending in this case for trees?

All summer I thought it over working in the Woolworth's on Wilson, lying on the beach, reading in whatever breeze I could find in the front room, library books with plain red or green covers, I thought about it. What do you say to a man who tells you to make a sacrifice for your country? While I stared at bins of socks, brassieres, shelves of dusty toys and bottles of leg makeup, tired goldfish in their murky tanks, I wondered. I had nothing to say.

Now the moon hangs over the middle of the road, out of reach but sinking into the place where we'll meet it three days from now. A desert I have seen in movies, magazine pictures, pictures in my head where nothing ever stops moving like Ray's Model A's wheels and the little whistle that happens every time he breathes through his nose. I will hear this sound all my life. Ours.

Flo had heard the news from her mother, Mrs. de Maestri from the woman who lived next door to the Rigneys. I had seen so little of Tommy the past couple of years even before he'd gone and enlisted, I felt like it had happened to somebody I barely knew until this one bright afternoon—the last Saturday before school started—I see him out walking down Wolcott, his cane sweeping the sidewalk. I crossed to the other side. I couldn't think of one thing to say or walk past him not saying anything. When I got home I felt so bad I didn't mind Hazard starting in on me again. Don't you care about the rest of the country, a war means everybody has to pitch in not just the soldiers, don't you care about other people?

Tommy's hand warm and thick on my face on our walk last Sunday, our last Sunday walk.

I gave up. He wouldn't have given me a day's peace, not as long as I had something I cared for. That's why when Raymond came into my life I told Pa not a word. I knew the old man too well.

One month ago. Last week we kissed by the lake. Tonight, here, I want to kiss him again but he's in his own world staring into the road right now, hands tight on the wheel. If I reached out and touched his face right below the scar below his eye he might not even know I was here.

Then his hands on my legs stopped his stopping sudden his question sudden. When I close my eyes to our kiss, not quite this one but a road into a dark place but not this one changing all the time but slow but still staying flat, open, straight, wide while still we move on through it and onward southward by south by southwest.

The line stood still. The line moved. I went to work. I did my part. Before the first day I thought I'd be able to work with my eyes closed and become like Tommy but in that place the noise was such you could do nothing but dream wide awake paying attention to every move the line chose to make. When the first day ended Hazard met me at the gate saying You don't know the meaning of work, saying Lying down underground we used to dream of an eight-and-a-half hour day and getting paid to stand on our own two feet. I nodded for his words. I dreamed an end to the war from every fuse and shell we packed going to kill a thousand Germans, Japs, whole armies surrendering so I could leave the plant behind forever. I held the sickness the dreaming gave me down like I held back my tears from him the first day.

My dreams changed. In the rage of the machines I learned to hear a silent world caught in the silence coming to meet us at the end of this war. Nobody crying or shouting but lying down together in fields of blood and grass. I will go back to school where Tommy can work as the janitor. He'll push his broom till he comes to a wall, turn and push the other way. In the plant I've learned to make things that explode, at the end I would learn how to put them back together.

A picture of Hitler. WE SHALL HATE OR WE SHALL FAIL.

One every two hours and fifty minutes I chewed three sticks of Wrigley's a day.

A picture of this girl and her baby lying dead in the mud watched by Hitler. THIS IS THE ENEMY. Hitler or the mud?

Maybe the other girls on the line liked me, I don't know. The things that circled through my head I kept secret. I snapped my gum and made jokes about the foreman. He said I've read a guidebook from Uncle Sam so I know how to manage females, I'll treat you the same as men but not quite. Female workers are different, more patient and stable, honest and sweet and loyal and clean so we'll all get along dandy if you follow the rules, tie up your hair, smoke outside, get to work on time, back from lunch on time, ready for inspection at any time, talk about your jobs to a single living soul at no time (loose lips), stow the griping, and above all take care in your work so our unit can have the best safety record this side of Midway and I don't mean the airport. And even above that keep your minds on the war and the boys whose lives limbs and eyesights depend on your concentration. The man's job you're holding down till the man can get home and take over again.

And then what for us?

COME ON IN SISTER. Even in the bathroom they got us. Hitler, Mussolini, the emperor of Japan whose name slips my

mind, all three smiling: TAKE IT EASY, EVERY MINUTE
YOU LOAF HERE HELPS US PLENTY.

They started me out at fifteen dollars and eighty-five cents a
week. Later on, a little more. Of course most of it's gone for the
upkeep on the flat and trying to see we ate a little better but
after a while I started to save some out for me. Bought a nice
pair of sling-pumps and a decent blue dress for nights out with
Flo and Thelma, nothing fancy but better than I ever had worn.
These things are in the suitcase now along with ma's picture,
along with the green dress I made myself and the war bonds I
saved up for. Not the music box which I left in my bottom
drawer for him to find some time or not. The bonds we can put
aside for our children when they happen after Raymond and I
lie down in a field of grass. Does it grow in Arizona? Lie down
on a narrow bed which I can't picture or the room. Ours. Under
a moon cutting through our roof, the moon waiting for us in the
desert.

"Dear Papa . . . The light through my window . . ."

While he'd sit next to me reading the war in the evening
paper I tried to sleep but never got farther than a kind of
not-waking where the movement of the bus became the
movement of the line became all of us marching in the door of
the plant. Becomes the movement of these wheels became all of
us getting off in the Loop and walking down the gray stairs into
the subway. If I couldn't get a seat I can sleep standing up home,
rocked by the slow slide of the el.

Now sleep's anyplace but in this car. As long as this night lasts
I want to be awake, eyes open or closed, hear his breathing to
know without looking he's there. Here.

"Sure is a lot of night."

He nods, tapping the wheel. "Can't argue with you there.
Same as the two sailors out on deck one day looking down on
the ocean, you follow me? And one of them says, Gee there sure

is a lot of water, and the other one goes, Yeah and that's only the top of it."

At least he doesn't laugh.

In the dark of morning the el still went rattling by pa and me sitting at the window munching our fried bread. Where can the likes of us buy a new toaster in this day and age? The el's echo drowned what little we had to say to each other. Those wheels against these. Those win, louder, higher pitched, falling and rising and rising to turn past and past the vacant lot, these so quiet it's a wonder we don't both fall asleep, him at the wheel and me poking myself to talk to him but what's to say for now? We said it all last week. Now all to do is wait for morning in the right town for stopping and changing ourselves over. October. The mornings come later.

The mornings grew lighter and the evenings till by the second week in June high daylight hung over our bus home. By then I had started reading the paper too for the invasion. I could read each column twice over while he did once. The war might end soon. I had worked this job less than a year already I could picture no end to it. Go back to school? I couldn't see myself except in those working dreams where Tommy played the first blind janitor ever. Anyway the war didn't end. By fall when they asked Hazard to work the night shift he said no he had to be home nights to make sure I stuck to his rules, home by eleven, nobody over. I pointed out I hardly went anywhere, just with Flo and Thelma, never stayed out late. His boss pointed out his duty. He switched to nighttime. Now I've known the freedom to ride home alone and walk in on an empty flat, not have to live my life inside his. My first night free I poured out a shot of rye from the bottle in his closet. Why does he hide it, thinking I'd give him a temperance lecture?

Flo and Thelma graduated from Grimm, Thel went to work at Carson's in the Loop where her big sister April modeled dresses and Flo helped out in the butcher shop now that Lou had gone off to the Pacific, and both of them started going out with sailors. I tagged along. They had a little money to spend and they knew guys willing to spend a little more. Flo and Thelma weren't victory girls but they knew how to go about persuading a guy to get them a pair of nylons, and often they didn't even have to come across. One night they came over with all the fixings to get me ready, to experiment on me. Plenty of makeup, even the better stuff, the hard-to-get. I'd never worn much knowing he'd only start a fight over it but they went to work and when they finished I had to admit I looked different but not even they could claim I looked much better what with my eyes too close together still and nose too long. Only so much you can do with an interesting face. Leaning over against Ray I aim the mirror at me. Not much you can do. Forget the lipstick, fix the mirror so the driver can see behind us again, but stay here a second leaning on his shoulder, a few seconds. Then I laughed and laughed till Flo checked my forehead for fever. Then Thel took out the home permanent set. They must have been there till one and when they left I wondered would I wake up bald.

I woke up nothing. Hazard sniffed the air when he got home and asked if all our eggs had gone rotten at once. Then he stared at my head till I told him to do what I was doing, pretend it was a dream. Brushing my hair a few thousand times I wondered why when Flo and Thelma get dolled up they look like younger smaller versions of Carmen Miranda and Martha Raye but when I did I looked like a sillier version of me.

And later when Thel's sister started bringing home some of the dresses and Thel loaned me one, the same: under that beautiful thing stood the same wide hips, small bust, bony shoulders and legs. Me.

Who captured this man anyway. But who knows what he's looking for? Is it me, am I your right move? I take his free hand. "Hey lady," he says, and smiling he works his fingers free.

I had fun going out anyway even if mine wasn't the same kind of fun as theirs. They were out to show these boys a good time and get what they could out of them. I went along to try and leave the rest of me behind in the flat and hear people talking without walls of noise between them, hear new music at the Avalon and dance myself half-asleep in the arms of some embarrassed sailor. And I wanted to experience the latest routine a guy could come up with for getting a girl to come across. Not that I ever gave in but in the a.m. I could tell Hazard that nothing had happened the night before and watch him not be able to make up his mind was I lying or not. Telling the truth and having him think it might be a lie put me one step ahead of him. Of course sometimes I was telling a lie about Thelma or Flo but not about me even if it was part of the war effort to give these kids what they wanted. My first time would be something better than a fast one with some boy who'd make me feel more alone than I already felt. Will be something better.

Only one boy got through to me at all, a kid from Iowa who sort of looked like Lew Ayres. Pa was glad Lew Ayres couldn't make any more pictures because a coward deserved no better and after that I liked Lew Ayres. This sailor was heavier set but had the same gentle eyes not like Tommy's wild ones in the old days or like Ray's tonight when he's so beat his eyes are slits. Gentle these were. Up till his fourth beer. Then he started cutting loose with a wave of words fouler than any I'd ever heard Tommy and Lou use when they'd try to outswear each other. Stow it, one of the other sailors said and then apologized for him: Calvin gets like this when he puts his fourth one away. Almost before I got it I lost my crush on Calvin from Dubuque but anyway where could we have gone? The back seat of a borrowed car was out, I wanted better and better than some stranger's rented room either. Could we go back to the flat, on my own bed, watched by the picture of ma? Calvin would have been long gone by the time pa got home but pa'd have known. Pa'd have smelled him.

We couldn't have gone anywhere. Maybe it's a good thing Calvin from Dubuque turned out to have such a foul mouth.

Is this the first light of sunup striking me now in the face or has the light been moving with us for miles while I slept? I don't remember sleeping, nor recall the end of the night.

"Ray? How about we pull over a few hours."

He starts whistling again, back and forth from "Sing Sing Sing" to "Boogie Woogie Bugle Boy."

"Raymond. Don't you need sleep?"

Suddenly he grins. "Not this guy."

This same light rises now over my father coming up the back stairs to the flat. "Dear Papa." Or he doesn't see the note at first only wonders if my alarm didn't go off and should he wake me. He sits down on his bed, lies back with his shoes still on in that sleepy light for just a second he'll close his eyes before going in to get me up for work.

"Hey, ever heard how you're supposed to keep both hands on the wheel?"

When I turn to look he doesn't even have one hand on, his left holds a cigarette and his right reaches out to brush a strand of hair out of my face letting the Model A sail along on its own control. Instead of shouting at his ways I turn again and let him stroke the back of my neck while I watch these brown and green hills come to life rising and falling like buildings far off through the windows of the el. Trees turning colors I never saw before. Why can't we stop here, make this place our home?

One by one we lost our jobs, one by one our replacements came home. I got mad waiting for my time. After we'd given two years to this work and some of the older women going on four now they could kick us out. Then when I thought about it some more I laughed and shrugged, what did I care if they let me go, what about all the hours and days I had wished the war over so I could get free?

But after they fired me what would I be part of?

I waited. Flo and Thelma stopped inviting me, all I could do was make wisecracks till the sailors started calling me Groucho and Thel said I spoiled their fun. I stayed home more, back in the front room with the radio—

"All Too Soon," that's the song came on the night he brought the radio home, that slow trombone sound floating across our hot front room—

And a book and the long call of Benny the nut man and the creak of his wheels rising to me from the street. What was I waiting for? In a short time, they told us, life will be better than ever before, the war in the Pacific over soon, as much meat as we wanted, coffee, bobby pins, long drives up the lake or into the country. Was I waiting for these better times? I don't know if I waited for anything.

Not Raymond Cope. I didn't see him in my dreams. In movies when a guy and girl fall at first glance they say they feel they've known each other forever. I don't feel that way and I bet Raymond doesn't either. We've got each other right now, why pretend there's more to it than that? If I dreamed a thing I dreamed Hazard and me getting along or at least talking now and then about something besides the price of a can of applesauce. What good would ending the war do if we went on living the same as before, him and me, all of us?

A bird, a shot of yellow and black whips out from a bush to our right and when Ray swerves to the left to miss it this bird cuts higher soaring out of sight beyond the trees on the far side and Ray pulls the car back into our lane smiling and shaking his head and gripping the wheel tight.

"Hell! Sleep's what we need."

As if he invented the idea.

But after he pulls off and we come to a clearing just out of sight of the road I can't drop off. I make him take the back seat, after all he's done the driving. When we get to Arizona he says he'll teach me. As much as you can lie down in a front seat I do and he gives me his jacket for a pillow but being crunched up is not what keeps me awake. My body could sleep and sleep in any posture, so light right now it hardly feels here. The stillness keeps me from sleep, stillness after a night of movement. movement.

Are there trees where we're going? Here surrounded by trees I can't name I can't find my way to sleep.

Ray's head rests on his arm his mouth open a little but his breathing almost silent this time and careful to make no sound I open the door. The air surprises me, not cold not for early morning not even with a wind the likes of which I've never heard. Each tree gives a different sound, the rattle of every pair of leaves clicking in its own time, the low moan of limbs turning and turning and a third sound a kind of whistling as if the leaves have holes.

Hazard's breathing when he sleeps. That whistle.

Down in the grass the stillness covers me again. The dew makes no sound even when I press my ear to the earth and close my eyes. Or here? Make this a place we can lie down in together?

Hazard breathing alone in his silent room. If he caught his daughter now what would he do to her? He catches his little girl once doing something she shouldn't. His wallet stinks of oil his pants oil slick coins. If she takes this penny down to the store will the lady know she stole it or not care these days people will take any penny comes into their hands. The girl can taste the candy already with the penny safe in her fist no pa here behind her his hand on the back of her neck freezing her twisitng her around in this hot room to face his wide palm hit me twice, on the hand that took the penny on the head that thought the deed. The second blow knocked me down. I couldn't even cry. He lifted me on to his bed then and pressed a cold cloth across my forehead while I lay watching his face turn and turn in the turning room watching mine. His mouth formed a promise never again never.

"What the hell, Vera?"

Ray's voice wakes me or was I sleeping or was I remembering? His voice, his shaking bring me back to wet cold grass under weak sun in morning air sharper now than when I lay down how long ago?

"How'd you end up out here?"

I put my arms around his waist and he lifts me on to my stiff legs, my damp skirt stuck with twigs and burrs clinging to my thighs.

"Did you see the hawk?" Ray says. "I saw him right when I woke up, like him being there woke me. Hovering. I just lied there waiting to watch him make his kill. But I never saw it happen. Blinked my eyes a couple times and that hawk was gone."

Raymond's words. Do you know yours is the face of a hawk, Raymond Cope? Do you know while we both slept the trees have stood us guard against hawks against all harm?

We get back in the car then. Half a mile down the road I'm still picking these burrs off my skirt and Raymond is saying we better find some gas soon or neither one of us is going to get married today. The longer I look for more burrs the more I keep seeing his face in that turning room so long ago the recalling makes me wonder what I have in common with the little girl. Nothing. She was scared all the time. Cold mornings she tries to lie perfectly still so she won't touch any part of the sheets that haven't been warmed in the night by her own body and won't let any cold air into the space between her body and the sheets.

One very cold morning she wakes more scared because she doesn't feel as cold as normal. Something wet warms her legs. She pulls back the cover crying out Pa she cries I'm bleeding.

But before he got out of bed and came in I wondered if maybe the blood was supposed to be a secret kids keep from grownups like dirty jokes or stealing a piece of fruit. I crawled back under the cover pulling it up almost over my eyes and while he stood there in the doorway I lay shivering watching him watch me. When he went away I figured he must not want to know. I smelled my blood secret safe.

On account of the worst snowfall in thirty-four years they called off school. I found Thelma out playing with the other kids. Would my blood trickle down and mark a trail in the white? When I pulled her aside and asked her was this our secret from grownups she laughed and took me home to her mother. Mrs. Reese did not laugh. I knew then it wasn't a secret kids kept from grownups but kids could laugh about it but grownups had to keep serious and make you lie down while they told you.

Later on I asked her Then is it a secret girls keep from their pa when he doesn't want to know anyway?

His face in the doorway past the cover pulled up over my mouth smelling my legs warm and wet. Never said a word and me neither never. His face wore the look I grew to know, wondering how had he got to this place left with a girl child the kind who bled in the sheets. I closed my eyes.

Opening them I close them again to a high room not mine with bed for two. Night or day? Through the only window a black sky full of pink stars giving light to an open field that might be a desert. Ray stands somewhere behind me in this place his eyes gone black watching me, waiting. The stars fly out from the sky, I turn to Ray my own voice saying Home. Home.

In the mirror my face looks old. I am old in a Missouri gas

station ladies' room. Not yet. But today I will be old in a Missouri hotel room. Now all I am is dirty tired hungry, young.

The sunlight shatters our fenders. The smell of gasoline and old tires and the sunlight alone are enough to take my hunger from me. Ray spreads Missouri open on the trunk. His finger points to the nearest town, blue on the white map on this brown car, a blue dot twenty twenty-five miles away.

Arrowhead Springs.

29 JUNE 1946 MR HAZARD HARKER 4718½ PAULINA STREET
CHICAGO ILLINOIS
DWIGHT RAYMOND COPE BORN 1:30 AM FIVE POUNDS
THIRTEEN OUNCES LOVE VERA

4. Opening Day

Where is Dwight when this old man wants water?

This old man. Even unspoken he likes the sound these words make. Old man, he played Ones. One crack running the width of the ceiling. On the bureau one snapshot of Vera alone. Early one morning, semi- turning to quarter-darkness through one window above the radiator facing gray southern sky and the limb of a bare elm. Damn the boy, he must have raised the shade. Bile rises to Hazard's throat when he turns in his damp bed to the cry from across the parking lot of the el at the end of this sleepopened night. A sound wheels make.

In the silence after the el has passed, his own breathing is too loud for sleep. The sound lungs make, unsound.

But he does sleep. Wakes. How long?

He smacks his lips as if the dryness of the sound will carry to the kitchen where the boy is clattering dishes and banging pots at a volume he can attain only when trying to be quiet. Today is the sixth to last day of the third to last month. Right? That many days plus three hours. Eleven a.m. in the morning. Unless the day proves too hot this old man will be there. Unless the CTA bus breaks down, unless the boy gets himself expelled, unless Hazard cashes in his chips in the meantime. Mean time. He turns his head back and forth on the pillow. Last through today, how many left then?

Don't start counting again. Ones only. One lamp, one rocker, one window facing west, one south. Light through the southern stronger now. Dwight should have left for school already. When he finally comes in with breakfast Hazard will tell him to shape up, straighten up, buckle down these last two months and seven days and. And to pull down the shades.

For now he'll shut out the Ones. Let his hands reach out to grasp two shoulders and move both his hands across her closing eyes into her hair, his two clumsy hands down her neck to her shoulders again and down. How long ago? Start counting. One afternoon, her, this room.

Forget that. Leave them lie, himself and her, however many afternoons ago.

One light.

Forget that night either.

The light of one torch in his muddy eyes. But many torches that night, one light here.

"Only me, Grampus."

Hazard squints. "Why the goddamn lamp?"

"The better to wolf your breakfast by."

Dwight props a pillow behind Hazard's shoulders and lowers the tray into the valley of the old man's abdomen. Orange slices, five, six, seven.

"No grapefruit at the Hi!Neighbor this week?"

Dwight clears his throat. "No, sir. Not even for ready money."

"What?"

"A play we read in English. They made a movie of it too but I haven't seen it yet."

Water never tastes as good as he imagines it will when he is lying in the dark unable to move. "All you ever say these days are lines from things. You don't even talk baseball anymore."

Dwight sits at the edge of the bed. "Sure I do. I'm going out there today, why do you think I haven't left for school?"

Hazard turns his head slowly to the window.

"Don't you know a snow is coming? Look at those clouds."

"Sure, that looks like a snow sky. But there can't be snow on Opening Day."

"Says who?"

"Me and Andre Rogers."

Hazard turns his eyes from the sight of that sky. "Pull down the shades. Says me."

Alone again, coffee cold and orange slices untouched, he tries to figure out why all of a sudden he has this urge to shave. This hunger. The day Alice shaved him he felt less hungry. In that room down by the stockyards, the only one she would know in Chicago, in the room where they could see their breath on the first of October he felt the blade in her sure hand against his cheek. The scent of potatoes from her long thin hand and the way her eyes narrowed when she pulled the blade along his jaw made his stomach feel less empty. Her hands had smelled of apples, now they smelled of potatoes, ammonia, the city.

It's the consumption, Mrs. Engle said, You'll have to move. He heard her voice from the hall as he lay in the corner of the dark room watching his own breath. Then he heard Alice's voice in response, deeper, quieter, that questioning tone. When she came back to him she pulled up the shade and by the afternoon autumn light and the life in her eyes she shaved him.

Life that went out when the third child came dead. Hazard tries to sit up, to put those lives away. To shave. Halfway up he lies back, exhausted. Often the first is lost. When the second survived but was a girl he lived for the third. The third would be a boy and grow up never hearing the wheels of skeleton trucks below, the wheels his father had heard every night to accompany his waking dream of Alice, above, in her night-gown. Night shift. Reaching for lumps of the black earth he dreamed her long fingers in daylight pulling apples from their limbs. While she turned over sighing in sleep he reached dreaming of her in the night shift. Wheels made the sound they make, the sound their son would grow tall never to hear. They made the sound Hazard heard every night till it came time for wives to lug buckets of water into houses to fill the tubs for their husbands' return. In her chapped hands she held the brush, scrubbing him down in early morning light or early morning darkness. One such morning she told him she was expecting again, the second, who would be Vera. Another she told him again.

But their son came dead in the room by the slaughteryards. Their son was in her the day she shaved him. What life it had she held in her steel blue eyes.

When the boy brings breakfast Hazard will tell him tales of grandmother gone days. In my days we never went late to anything. In my nights we showed up on time to work til our wives filled the buckets and made ready for our dirt, for us to come up from below with the sun. When the boy brings breakfast Hazard will tell him everything.

Dwight's been and gone. This old man lies alone. He sits up slowly and watches his feet sink toward the floor. When they touch he wonders why the floor isn't cold. Or have his soles lost their feeling? Not quite. They sense the floor but it feels like nothing solid. He stands anyway. He begins to count the steps it takes to reach the bathroom.

Leaning on his fists against the sink, staring into the mirror, he sees a few fat yellow snowflakes drift past the window behind him. Christ, on Opening Day!

Shalt not take His Name in vain.

Yes I can. Now I can. Take down this snapshot of Him on the Mount. Should have yesterday when Dwight woke me up to show me my birthday present. Blasphemy on blasphemy. The boy knows me too well.

He slips the picture card into his heart's pocket.

On pajamas a heart's pocket must be for holding picture cards of the Sermon on the Mount.

In the mirror the flakes look so fat and fall so slowly he imagines he is only imagining them. He turns. They are there, on Opening Day. So the boy was wrong, the wise guy. Coughs of laughter shake him at the image of his grandson in the right-field bleachers watching this snow settle into the outfield grass. The kid who's too smart to want to make anything of himself. Not even completely a kid anymore, a kid was when he'd sit watching Hazard shave, those big dark eyes following every move. Old eyes. Where had a child's eyes acquired such wisdom? They bored into you, asking questions you couldn't even grasp much less answer. So seldom a word spoken. A week might pass in which the old man heard no more than "Bye Grampa" when Dwight left for school, "Hi Grampa" when Hazard came home from the plant, and "Okay" or "Sort of okay" when Hazard asked how school had gone. In between, long silences. Is this what having a boy was supposed to be like? Well, you couldn't plan anything, least of all a daughter who seldom said a word and her son who took after her, watched you shave, and stares at you now, a silent boy-stranger.

That boy is gone now. Into Dwight gone days.

The old man rubs his brush into the cracked wedge of soap at the bottom of his cup and watches lather begin to form. Shaving will fill his morning, cure his hunger.

When the doctor told Hazard that his grandson had a slight heart murmur the old man thought, The boy's heart does more talking than he does. When the school people called to say they wanted to test Dwight to see if he could skip first grade Hazard laughed into the phone. How could they tell a kid was smart if he never spoke, did they go by the wise look in his eyes? Or maybe at school Dwight turned into somebody else and talked and talked until the school people decided to move him up in hopes of shutting his trap.

How'd those tests go today?

Okay, I guess.

Over supper a few days later: They ever tell you how you came out on those tests?

Oh, I'm supposed to move up to second grade on Monday.

What would they have had to say to each other these ten years if baseball had never been invented?

The Red Mask of Death. Dwight has told him about some kind of movie one of these nights lately, keeping him awake, going on and on in that anxious voice. This face in the mirror is Hazard's own handiwork, he has been shaving without paying attention to the blooming of these bubbles, points of red in a field of gray. At least they prove he is still alive. Why did he want to shave in the first place, didn't he know he would still feel hungry?

An el is moving by beyond the parking lot but when he stands on the stool to look out at the snowfall he begins to cough, and coughs long and loud enough that the el seems to pass noiselessly. Later he can hear the slap of flakes, eight, nine, ten, melting as soon as they hit the window. The same snow falls on Wrigley Field. Hazard wants to laugh again at the stubborn boy out there in the bleachers but he realizes now that he himself will have no game to listen to. Nothing to mark the afternoon's drift, no way to divide a certain three hours of his last days into nine innings, half-innings, into batters, pitches, waits between, a dumb series of sounds and numbers and outs and remembered plays and remembered waits. This afternoon will be a One.

Someone watches him rub witch hazel into his cheeks. Turning, he is alone, his daughter not there in the doorway where she'd watch him shave, staring the same way her son would. Her eyes, her son's. Four, watching the old man's hands frozen against his face, caught in this moment by two child-strangers not there. Christ's eyes, looking out from the heart's pocket. Alice's, narrowing down at him. A yellow multitude of eyes framed by torches in the frozen night will watch him come back to life.

Now the old man is starving. Switching off the light he stumbles out so quickly he can't even feel himself brush past the child-stranger in the doorway.

He warms his face in the slow heat rising from the toaster coils.

"Four. Five. Six."

When he reaches twenty-nine he will push up the lever and the toaster will offer a perfect piece, hot enough to melt butter even in this kitchen but not burned, not the color and taste of coal. "Ten." A sound wheels make. The coal truck is pulling up in front of the storeroom. The old man would go to the window and look down at the alley, at the gray snow settling into the load of coal, but he has to remain at his post.

Why can't we get a decent toaster, she'd ask. One that works all the time instead of this contraption. She was right. It never worked for more than a few weeks at a time, then it would refuse to toast the bread at all or else would leave you with a charred hunk of what she called "ex-bread." Then Hazard would take out a screwdriver and poke around until he got things working again for a while.

But damn it to hell, where had she come by the trace of resignation in her voice, in her small eyes and the set of her mouth? There had to be some wish to get back at him for not doing right by her, even if he didn't know how he had done wrong. After all, the toaster worked a lot of the time, didn't it? With Hazard's help it lasted right through those years when nobody who wasn't somebody could buy a new toaster, until one December morning it burst into half-hearted flames. And this new-fangled pop-up kind the old man bought that Christmas at the Salvation Army, this one has worked just fine in its own way, with Hazard's help. Who knows but that Dwight might get a second decade's use out of it after this old man moves on?

But soon Dwight will be able to buy the best toaster in Chicagoland. Come high school graduation. U.S. Savings Bonds. Bonds that save but not like Jesus. If Jesus does. Which the old man has given up wondering once and for all.

The boy's father left him nothing but a heart murmur. His mother left him a future, bonds, for when he graduates.

He hears the roar of coal in the alley, he holds to his post, counting, and when the back doorbell rings he hears it as if it were ringing on a summer day twelve, thirteen years ago. "Nineteen," he counts. Afternoon, summer, he stood puzzling over Vera's words, and on the second ring he opened the back door.

When you didn't answer the first ring I thought maybe you weren't home, Patrice said. Did Hazard smile at her standing out there or did he only shake his head and say, No I'm right here. He put Vera's letter down on the kitchen table. He let Patrice in.

When the doorbell rings a second time he hears it in the present. "Hell and creation." Cursing the doorbell makes him lose count. He curses again.

The eyes of the young man on the landing are pearls of ice. Wondering when he last breathed fresh air, Hazard begins to shiver. "Yeah?"

"Samuels Brush Company, sir. Hope I'm not disturbing you."

"Why aren't you in school?"

"Spring break from Loyola, sir."

This fairhaired broadshouldered boy who has come out in the cold to make a few extra bucks on his break, this young man with a winning smile, calm and sure and eager, is the opposite of Dwight. He has been tramping through the April snow and still his shoes hold their shine.

His shoes. Dwight's.

"Looks like you put your own product to good use."

"Our shoeshine kits are as efficient as you'll find."

"I believe in a shined pair of shoes."

The old man wonders what his own words mean, but the boy seems to understand. "I'm with you. Shoes make the man."

Hazard mumbles, "Hang on," and steps back, bumps into the table, turns, expecting to find the half-read letter from Vera, instead finds that the toaster is now giving out brown smoke, and lunges for the hoard of bills inside the Yogi Bear cookie jar.

"Hang on," he says again. Back at the door he pushes a ten-dollar bill through the sharp air at the surprised face of the boy, whose smile is now so bright it makes the old man dizzy.

He held Patrice, lies now alone, covered with his hands her smooth face, turns slowly on his side trying slowly to take a breath, moved his wide hands clumsily down the back of her neck and down. The smell of burned toast drifts in from the kitchen. She wouldn't look at him. Moving his hands along Patrice's broad back he saw smoke float from a frying pan into Alice's steel blue eyes the morning she told him she was expecting again. Who would be the son who would never. He crouched in the tub in the middle of the room. Patrice would not look at him. This son will live, Alice said, smoke rising toward her eyes. Moving his hands through the space where Patrice lay beside him he wonders how old Patrice was that day. Hazel eyes that wouldn't look at him, thirteen, no, twelve years ago, summer days, the summer he went to get Dwight. Her swollen hands. Arthrytis. She spelled it for him. What does it matter how old she was? All that matters was the somewhere else look in her eyes, the bead of sweat that slid down her

temple, the slow rocking of her short heavy body. Not like
Alice's which had lain long and narrow and light in his clumsy
arms. Her eyes not like the light in Alice's following close the
movement of her own hand scraping the razor along his jaw.
Always that questioning tone in her voice. Mrs. Engle thinks
you have the consumption and says we'll have to leave? The
questioning in her voice told him she thought she could
persuade the landlady to let them stay. In that voice she made
even bad news sound like cause for hope. While her hand drew
the razor beneath his chin. While their son grew dead inside her.

In that room her silence told him she was dying. No more
space for questions. Third one, dead, second son, that was that.
He told Vera to take off her shoes so as not to break the silence.
Was that when the resignation had come into the girl, in the
silent room where she waited for nothing she could understand?
Where Hazard waited for Vera's mother to finish dying, for the
time, which came soon enough, when he and she would be left
alone together, when he would take on the raising of the
daughter alone.

The picture she sent him looking out the back door of her
house, hers and her sometime husband's, why recall that picture
now, why can he see that view of the desert so clearly? Each
grain of Arizona sand a separate and perfect thing on the
smooth almost white desert floor. Why that picture now? He
sent her the music box. In her thank-you letter she enclosed this
picture from out her back door. He found the music box in
someone's trash, and even though the tune sounded as if the
ending had been left out he brought it home and wrapped it up
for Christmas. When she brought it back from Music Appreciation class and said it was from a symphony by Hidin, Hazard
asked what was he hidin' from. Instead of laughing she spelled
out the name for him: H-y-d-e-n—was that it? Where is the
music box now and why didn't he find it among her things in

that house? It always stopped a few notes from the end and then she'd hum the rest of the tune as her teacher had whistled it for her.

That same winter—was it?—the morning came when she woke him calling, Pa, Pa there's blood. He went to her room. She hid herself. She closed her eyes. He went away. Not a word spoken. At some point every day he sees again the closing of her eyes just as he sees the light by which his wife once shaved him and again the distant gaze of the only woman to lie with him in this room. Twelve summers ago, when Dwight arrived in this old man's life and Patrice stopped lying in this old man's bed. Now with each turn of his head back and forth on the damp pillow he hopes to shake himself free of Patrice's gaze, Alice's light, his daughter hiding herself from him, send them to their rest, himself to his own. The faces remain, neither wholly present in this room bound by cracked walls and by windows streaked with dirty snow nor simply turning through the remembered sound of el wheels or factory wheels or skeleton truck wheels but in between, nowhere, not subject to his wish that they leave him lie.

How many eyes watch him now? He tries to count Ones. In the ceiling, not one crack now but several, a river with creeks. The pockmarks, bubbles, indentations on each wall are many more than he can count. By the southern window grows the shape of a lizard, over the bureau the shape of a cow's skull. Did he see the skull of a cow from the train window, no, but did he see it riding into Centinela or riding away with the boy, but no, back to Chicago, but no. Seeing his daughter's snapshot again beneath the shape of the skull he closes his eyes. The letter he was reading when Patrice came to the back door lies in the bottom drawer with all her letters, the telegram of Dwight's birth, the note she left under the family portrait in her bedroom. Every letter of every word of every letter, how many characters in that bundle beneath sweaters and flannel shirts no longer worn? How many *m*'s, *r*'s, *f*'s, *a*'s, commas, question marks? Infinite would mean you could never read them all and he has followed every curve and slash and then folded them up and retied the bundle and put them away too many times. Long ago he should have burned them, freed himself from the words and the fear of Dwight one day finding the words. This simple thing still undone.

When he opens his eyes the letters of the alphabet are plastered to the wall in her handwriting, her way of crossing a *t*, the backward *e* she sometimes made. Vera's alphabet repeats itself countless times along the creeks, in the cow's eyes, replacing the flakes at the windows. An infinity of letters.

Close them. Keep them closed until the letters go away.

His first prayer. This morning before sleep he can feel the men of the day shift moving beneath him. He has worked nineteen years today. He doesn't pray to be allowed to live through nineteen more years or one more but to be delivered from the mine before the twentieth is out: a cave-in, or inherit a million bucks from an unknown great-granduncle in Alaska, or find the guts or craziness to say No to going down one night. He doesn't care how. Only deliverance.

Who is it he prays to? He doesn't know. This morning just before sleep both the older Hazard and the younger at once are smiling, drifting near sleep, Chicago, April, nineteen sixty-three, Musil, late winter, nineteen twenty-nine. Both beds are full of the longing living in Hazard at age thirty-three and the certainty that is his at sixty-eight. The old man repeats the prayer, the young holds the old man's death in his lungs and smiles at knowing the first prayer will be answered: next winter comes the shutdown, next winter the shacks will fill with men in shock at finding their bodies clean of even the deepest dirt. Their boots will shine for days and then they will polish them once more. In shock the men will watch their children begin to starve. Alice and he, at last in bed at the same time for night after night, will listen all night to Vera, three, three-and-a-half, cry in hunger. His prayer answered, he will go out and stare down the road west. His sleep begun, he offers a smile to a God, a Jesus, to whoever could answer his first prayer.

One weight, never felt before, presses his chest. No weight pressed his chest when he lay below, trapped. One weight pressed his leg, another his arm, none his chest, that night when he lay on his side in the mine waiting to die. Today while he lies on his back waiting for nothing or to die or for the chance to breathe beyond this weight he knows the weight can only press him in his mind. In the mind, in the mine.

If it doesn't press me down then why can't I? Open them and see no weight then breathe again. Open them! Why can't?

Leave him lie. Him, them all. The earth gave way because they were meant to trap themselves. No surprise there. Expect nothing, Papa taught us and then at least you won't be dismayed. One by one we went below with him, Lemuel, Seth, me last. No truck with the union because the union taught you to expect something. Before the union got strong a man knew where he stood. Where he crawled. Through a place where you knew to expect nothing.

God but this weight, this way, these years, of dying. Go ahead, save him after all. Me. Dig me out. Bring him water and cover him till the wagon comes. Mend him so he can go back down. Open, lift, open.

No weight presses him. He knew all along and sees for certain now in the fading light of his own room, in its quiet, perfect but for the sound wheels make. He takes a breath, or something like one. The wheels must be a rush-hour el, in winter this room is about so dark at rush hour.

Not winter. Snow today but April, later than rush hour, evening. Opening Day, and Hazard has spent every bit of it in bed without dreaming one thing he can remember.

The wheels have given way to a ringing sound, which stops, begins again, probably a phone in the Duttons' place across the hall or maybe right here. He can't tell. He has spent a whole day without dreams or if there were he can't recall them. If he is careful he won't have to.

By the southern window grows the shape of a lizard in the plaster. On the morning after a whole night of no dreams he woke on their hide-a-bed, what was their name, and a lizard sat atop the radio glinting dark green under the watchful gaze of a crow in the lone tree in their front yard. The Whalens. But no lizard, he had only dreamed it. But no dreams so how could he? A lizard or not, if he is careful he won't remember for sure, won't remember that morning or the dreams of the night before. He has read somewhere that everyone dreams every moment of sleep, that particular night could not have been dreamless. Nor could this past day. But if he stays lucky or careful he won't recall a single picture.

Careful has nothing to do with it. The dreams will come back to him anyway. They have their way of sliding from his hands in the moment when he realizes himself awake and still alive, but hours or weeks later at some point when he imagines himself dead they wash over him as if to prove he hasn't died because a dead man can't be washed in the pictures of his own dying and still know they are only pictures. For his own death is all he can dream anymore. Dwight's hands planting daisies by his grave. Count on the boy to plant the wrong flowers for mourning! But the old man's grave is right beside Vera's. How did Dwight find out where his mother was buried? At the end Hazard must have let it slip out. After all, he promised when the boy grew up he would tell. But now is too soon, the boy is still a young fool in dirty shoes who kicks heavy dust over the flowers and the letters of his mother's name, grandfather's name, the fool, smiling his slightly crooked smile and pressing his shoes into the gravedirt.

The old man places his hand around the glass of water on the bedside table but can't begin to lift it. Inside the glass the graveflowers are dying of heaviness. The old copies of *Popular Mechanics*, every object in this room, is much too heavy. Even the branches scrape the window with an unbearable weight. The light is being pushed back by the dark, unbearably slowly, the evening gathers the heavy dumbness of the day, the dumb weight of memory. If he had the strength to open the bottom bureau drawer memory would leak out on his hands in pearls of ink. If he could lift the glass the water would spill in pearls, each the same because every sight held in his mind, in the mine, is the same. Standing in the hall reading the telegram of Vera's death means exactly as much or as little as finding a St. Louis Cardinals souvenir ring in a box of Nabisco Shredded Wheat before going to work one Monday morning in the spring of 1947. That discovery carries no less force than the feel of the scrub brush in Alice's hand against his back or of Patrice Rigney's wide shoulders in his arms; his father's smell of whiskey and tobacco; the abashed look on Dwight's face one morning three years ago when he told Hazard at breakfast that from now on he would do his own laundry, including his sheets. Each memory, each pearl, feels, looks, and sounds as dull, heavy, and forgettable as every other. But unforgettable. Must be forgotten, impossible to forget. If he lies here long enough they will crush him; slowly, but they will press what life is left from his lungs. If he is lucky.

When the ringing comes again and again he reaches through all that air. The plaintiveness in Dwight's voice startles him.

"Grampa? You awake?"

Hazard sighs. What answer can he give to such a question?

"I mean, I called a few minutes ago, I let it ring a dozen times."

"Unh."

"You must know it's me, I can tell by the joy in your voice."

"Uh-huh."

"You're not going senile on me now, are you?"

"I wish my memory would go on strike, but no such luck."

"I thought you didn't believe in strikes."

Ha, ha. "You still at the ballpark?"

"It's seven at night, Hazard. They called the game eight hours ago."

"Don't call me Hazard. So you went to school instead?"

"Are you joshing me? I can't show up that late without a note from you. How about tomorrow?"

"How about it?"

"Will you write one?"

As if the boy is right in front of him Hazard shakes his head. "Sure. I'll write you played hookey to go watch the Cubs have a snowball fight."

"Look out the window now and then, Grampus. The snow melted."

"Maybe it'll warm up enough to have Opening Day tomorrow."

"Yeah, but I can't ditch two days in a row, not if I want to graduate."

"Since when do you want to?"

"Oh, it's just to please my grandfather. He wants to see one Harker finish high school."

The boy's smile: Hazard can hear it, and behind the silence

that settles between them he can hear the slow wheels of his grandson's evening world, a phone ringing, two or three typewriters, a distant call: "Boy!" Is this what Dwight wants, never to get beyond running messages? The old man listens to his own breath whistling back to him. "Late again tonight?"

"No, I made my trip to the Drake this afternoon. Two Ida Lupinos, *On Dangerous Ground* and this other one with Bogart called *High*—"

"Since when do you spend your afternoons in that place?"

"Well, I couldn't show up at Grimm. Anyway the Drake's a whole nother world in the daytime. I hardly ever see a woman there at night, but today I saw quite a few."

"Hoors."

"That's right, Hazard, hoboes and hoors. I've got to go, time for coffee with Mr. Sheffield."

"Go easy with the coffee."

"I'll see you."

Coffee with Sheffield. Tomorrow when he brings breakfast he'll have some new piece of communistic bunkola: The important thing is to stop caring, or, The end of the world doesn't seem like such a bad idea, or, Who nominated America for Promised Land? How bad off does a grown man have to be to say such things to a kid as impressionable as Dwight? But no point warning the boy. Anyone fool enough to sit in the snow at Wrigley Field's beyond saving. Any boy with so little ambition he can listen to such raving deserves whatever he hears.

He hangs up, at last. Why let the boy stir up old tired rage? Before the phone rang he was starting to feel a moment's peace, a settling. Weight of years closing in on him, but a release. The release brought by all that weight. To set him free.

But his end will not come so easily. If he wants it tonight he will have to seize it. Make the long slow walk to the bathroom, counting, five steps, six, eight, fumbling for the light switch, nine, for the medicine cabinet door, fumbling for his razor. Finish it here or bother taking the same number of steps back so he can die in his own bed? Easier for the kid, just sheets to toss in the incinerator, no blood to scrape off the sink or the toilet. For the kid's sake he will walk the nine steps back and stretch out before placing the razor to his throat.

He lies back on top of the sheets. In his hand the razor feels almost too heavy, of course, but having carried it this far he knows he can raise it the few inches that remain.

For once when he closes his eyes he can see nothing. This is what release should be. He starts to take a breath.

The old man's eyes are open. Why the shoes? If every remembered sight means as little as every other, why did a certain one come to him this morning when he glanced at the shined shoes of the salesboy? This remembering itself is cause for wonder. He hasn't spent all day in bed, at some point he must have taken steps, shaved, lost count of the toaster so he could talk to a boy standing in the cold beyond the back door. The sight that came to him then was of another pair of brown shoes, much smaller than those of this boy but, like his, polished to a fine gleam. He held out real cash for a shoeshine kit so his daughter's child could look at least partway decent at his high school graduation, decent from the ankles down. A graduation present to go with the bonds. Two months, five days, how many hours? One day less in the reckoning. When he finishes, his breath is almost a real one.

Even more slowly he gets out of bed once more. From the closet he takes the thing he found beside his bed when he woke yesterday morning. It stood there pointing serenely at its own heart. He carries this large plastic Jesus to the same spot now. With the same unbearable slowness he plugs it in. On his night table the razor gleams. He crawls back into bed. Before him the heart begins to flash on and off. Yesterday morning, while the old man lay there staring at this piece of junk Dwight said, "Thought this might cure you of your Jesus binge."

He was right. Hazard won't read aloud to himself from the Gospels anymore. He took down—today? yes!—the picture card of the Sermon on the Mount. What business does he have dealing with such things? Having spent this long as nothing, not even an honest to goodness atheist, how did he imagine he could demand that the Lord come suddenly into his dying life? Dwight saw through it. Dwight knew where the praying and reciting and the picture cards came from. Yesterday morning when Dwight stood at the foot of the bed watching his grandfather watch the statue, the old man knew this stranger could see inside him. Thought this might cure you. Get that contraption out of here, the old man said, pretending to be mad instead of scared, scared of this boy's way of knowing him. Get it out of my sight. But now he is relieved. No more being watched by those picture card Jesus eyes every time he goes to the bathroom. No more trying to make sense of all the contradictions the evangelists, or God, loaded into the New Testament. This blinking heart is comfort enough, or will have to be. Leave the rest lie. Let the here and now offer a sound to wring the whole pain of taking a breath from your lungs.

Under a damp sheet the old man lies, under the sound an el makes, metal on metal, fading, returning, gone. The silent heart blinks. He lies waiting for the sound, five hours from now, of the el bringing Dwight home. He won't know which el until the key turns in the door. Then the old man will say, All right, it was that one, the sound those wheels made.

He lets the dim heart blink, once, once, once, once.

△ △ △

June 30
Pa,

Dwight celebrated his first birthday yesterday. From the telegram last year you might have figured out he came a little early and he's still on the small side now but the doc says he'll be fine. As far as smarts go he seems to have gotten his share and then some. The only real bad thing was his blood. All of it had to be taken from him to be replaced by a healthy body's worth and he probably stood up to that better than I did. Everything's fine now.

I just thought you might want to know.

Vera

June the 25th

He must be going on three. Why don't you send me a picture?

Hazard Harker

PS. I am fine. I guess.

5.   Other People's Lives (1)

"Right out of high school this boy runs away from home. Chicago holds nothing for him anymore. He's saved a little from his after-school job, enough to get him by Greyhound to New York or Hollywood. But he's had enough of city lights for a while, he gets off the bus at—"

"Des Moines?"

"No, even Des Moines is too much of a city. The young man wants a small town. Main street, general store, filling station, movie house. Diner."

"One movie house?"

"The town is that small. But at least the bill changes every week. You're used to it changing every day, but he's looking for a slower pace."

In the window Dwight sees reflected the steam rising from their cups toward the bare bulb overhead. He has to press his face against the glass to make out the still forms of cars in the alley. Then he can see the figure of a woman in a gray raincoat pass through the fine rain, her high heels clicking faintly.

"Any girls in this town?"

"I'm getting to that," Sheffield answers. "This boy isn't only searching for a girl. He's after something else he can't quite put a name to."

"Adventure."

"That's close. But not gangsters or buried treasure. An adventure of being alone and seventeen with nothing to do on a summer night."

"I know," Dwight says. "Back when I had my nights free I used to love just walking the streets. If I had met the girl of my dreams I would have thought—what was it Lou Gehrig said? *I consider myself the luckiest man on the face of the earth*—but even knowing I wouldn't meet her I loved the streets themselves."

"Bright or dark," Sheffield says.

"Empty or crowded."

"But the strange thing is, this boy does meet her. He takes a job at the filling station right across from the Metro Diner: Three Square Meals A Day. At noon he looks up from pumping two bucks of regular into somebody's Nash to see this girl in white show up at work. For days he thinks of her that way, the Girl in White. Lunchtime he eats a sandwich out in the field behind the station but in the evening he walks across the street for his supper. This is July, hours of light still left. When he turns around on his stool at the counter he can watch the town turn even more peaceful. He does that a lot, to keep from watching her too much. He calls her the Girl in White because she's his age, young enough to be called a girl, and because her black hair and dark eyes make the uniform stand out. One night he follows her home."

"Wait. Doesn't he talk to her?"

"Not yet, except to order his supper. Afterward he wanders the streets before returning to his room over the station. But this one night he waits at the corner behind a Chinese elm and watches her lock up and come down Water Street and when she turns he follows this white figure along one lane and then another. Of course he can stay pretty far behind because she's in white but even so he wonders if she might hear him, the streets are so quiet. Only a screech owl to break the night and from halfway across town a dog howling at the three-quarter moon. But she never looks back."

"Maybe she doesn't want him to know she knows."

"Maybe. Then she stops at a huge pale blue house with

yellow trim, three stories plus attic, a little dead-end street where he hears nothing but the tap of her shoes up the walk. Later there's a light on the third floor, later still it goes off. On the way home he hears the tips of branches scrape the sides of dark houses."

"This is July, right? Next month, you mean?"

Sheffield gets up to fill their cups again. "Right out of high school. And you get out—"

"In two weeks." Watching the coffee rise in his cup he realizes this will be his third, he'll have trouble sleeping again. He doesn't mind. Drinking coffee is one of Sheffield's ways of not drinking anything else.

"You ought to forget these late-nighters with me," Sheffield says. "Get some rest now and then."

"If I wasn't here I'd be at the Drake."

"At least that's educational."

"So is this," Dwight says, and gets up for some half-and-half. When Sheffield says, "Tell me the title of the first movie you ever saw," Dwight stands so long at the open refrigerator, wondering, that the man speaks again: "I know the frigidaire needs defrosting, but not tonight."

Dwight gets the half-and-half and lets the door close. "Sorry."

"Forget it."

"No, I mean about my first movie. I do forget. Isn't that terrible? I remember riding all the way down to Phoenix, and maybe that was a first time too, and going for a root-beer float after. And the fake Egyptian decorations. But not the movie."

"Your mother took you?"

Dwight nods. "And when we came out I couldn't believe there was still daylight. I must've thought the whole world would be dark from then on." He pours half-and-half. "He moves into her rooming house?"

"No, living across from her would be too close. But the next night while she's ringing up his check he says, I followed you home. He says it so softly she doesn't hear him. When he repeats himself the words come out so loud the man at the end of the counter looks up, and he's hard of hearing. The waitress only says, Be careful.

"This time when she leaves he comes right up to her and asks if he can walk her home. She looks around as if wondering where the danger is supposed to be coming from, and says, Fine.

"Tonight there's hardly a breath of wind to cover his own heartbeat or footsteps while he tries to think of things to say. At first she isn't even impressed that he comes from Chicago. But then he sketches a summer night in the city for her, with a breeze slipping in off the lake and the stars competing with the lights of Michigan Avenue."

"Are you kidding? Women fall for lines like that?"

"This one does, in this story. Every night for a week he walks her home."

"Sometimes," Dwight says, "he gets so nervous he tells a stupid joke, the kind he used to read in *Boy's Life*: Why can't you ever starve to death in the desert?—Because of the sand which is there!"

"Boy. He must be really nervous to tell that one. But finally gets up the gumption to ask her out to that movie theater. Fixes himself up, a clean shirt, Brylcreem, you name it."

"I don't use Brylcreem, or any of that stuff."

"He never has, either. The movie turns out even better than he expected. Have you seen any Nicholas Ray?"

"I think just one," Dwight says. "It's only lately I started noticing the director's name. *In A Lonely Place*."

"Well, he notices. After the movie, over a root-beer float he's telling her about this way the director composes some of his shots, and suddenly she points out something entirely different, something, say, about how the woman keeps putting her trust in the man but he won't trust her until it's too late. This is not something a movie buff would necessarily catch, but someone who paid attention to people would. The boy is knocked out, he's never looked at a movie as being about people. Walking her home he says not a word, only studies her face in the changing shadows. When they get to the boarding house gate, where they always say good night, she tells him to take his shoes off so her landlady won't hear his footsteps into the house with her.

"At dawn he leaves her asleep and walks and walks. Every street leads to a corn field or a pasture. The streets and the countryside fill up with milky light. By the time he gets back to the filling station it's opening time and he's exhausted, all day he can barely go through the motions. When he shows up at the cafe he can't understand why she won't meet his eyes, or why when they reach the boarding house she only says Good night. He grabs her arm, he wants to know what's going on. She says, You left me alone, I woke up alone, and in the end you'll move on.

"The next morning he wakes up in his own tiny room and goes down to the field behind the gas station, where at the far edge the field starts to merge with a swamp, and picks wild irises. He makes a kind of rough bouquet, tied with twine, and leaves it behind the counter of the cafe. That night he waits in his room, eating something tasteless out of a can, and when he sees her locking up he goes down. She's carrying the flowers. Thank you, these are very nice, she says. And then she tells him her life."

The man gets up suddenly and starts fixing another pot of coffee. "This whole pot's for me, you've had too much already." He starts humming the theme from "Perry Mason."

"I'm fine," Dwight says. His hands are shaking slightly and his eyes burn. Why doesn't Sheffield put up a shade around that bulb? The boy studies the ugly picture of a ship on the wall over the stove, then the equally ugly one of another ship over the closed rolltop desk. Over the cot in the corner is a third picture, ugly in a different way. The other two probably came from Goldblatt's, but this one, unframed, its canvas torn along one edge, must have been painted by someone Sheffield knows. Why would he keep it otherwise?

In a dark room high above the lights of downtown Chicago seven men are sitting around a conference table. Those lights, yellow and sharp white, are the only bright colors behind the dark brown of the long table, blacks and grays of their suits and ties, their pale flesh. Their dead eyes stare at the brown blood seeping from their throats and wrists. Each time he comes up here Dwight wants to ask Sheffield, Why do the men bleed? What are they doing in this conference room in the middle of the night? Where did the picture come from? He turns to find Sheffield watching him study the picture.

"So then what happens?"

Sheffield bends to light his cigarette at the stove. "Then he learns a little about this Girl in White. She grew up on a small farm. The farm went under, her father ran off, the family came apart. She ended up here. Every week she goes to visit her mother, dying in the county hospital thirty miles away. The girl wants to get away but doesn't know how. She says, There's nothing out of the ordinary about me. He never tells her how much he disagrees.

"The rest of the summer they take these walks, or sometimes go to the movies, and usually they end up back in her room. The faded wallpaper with its flowers turning endlessly into other flowers begins to haunt him. He wakes early and lies there watching those pale petals come into view, waiting for her to awaken.

"You know you'll leave me, she keeps saying, That's how these things end. He says, I won't move on, but in himself he doesn't know. The mornings grow cooler, the wallpaper comes later into sight, and by the time the leaves have begun to change the girl's mother is dead. The girl says, She never got more than thirty miles from the house where she was born, the woman stays behind and the man leaves. The boy says, I don't know but it can't always be that way.

"And then one day . . ."

He puts out his cigarette.

"Go on," Dwight says.

"You go on."

"Me?"

Sheffield gets up to catch the coffee from boiling over. "You tell the rest."

Dwight laughs. "It's your story."

"My beginning. You end it."

The boy sits up, looking down into the alley again. "Okay." Then he looks out the window some more. "Okay. Let's say she's the one. This one morning he wakes up and, well, this would be around the middle of October, it's all dark when he wakes up and this time he's alone. Instead of her lying next to him there's just a note on the pillow—*I'm sorry but I had to be the one.* Or is that too corny?"

"Don't ask me. I think the whole story's pretty corny."

"Okay. He gets up. He walks back across town to work, and the smell of the pumps makes him sick. He can barely get through the workday."

"Hold on, you mean there's more to the story after she leaves?"

"It's coming to me. Something. It comes to him, while he's pumping gas, this idea. He runs across the street and tells her boss he can start work tomorrow, the noon shift. The boss thinks he's crazy—This isn't some French restaurant, I need a new girl. The kid goes, Come on! How soon will you find a new waitress in this town? I know the job, I sure as hell watched her do it enough times. I'll take less pay to start 'cause I'm not experienced but I want two meals a day here same as she got. The boss tells me I'll have to take a lot of wisecracks. I say, So will you, for hiring me.

"We shake hands. Then I go knock on the rooming house door—Understand there's a room vacant on the third floor. How do I know that, when the sign isn't out yet. I just know. Now can I have the room?"

Dwight holds up his cup. "I guess I will have one more."

"You guess you'll hit the road. Assuming that's the end of the story."

"That's all that comes to me."

In the small mirror over his dresser he watches his own hands strike the match and bring the flame slowly to the Chesterfield Regular between his lips. Charlie Witt claims non-filters make you sterile, but Garfield or Bogart never smoked anything but non-filters. Come to think of it, Dwight has never seen either of these men in the role of a father, but this couldn't be because they went sterile from non-filters. Maybe the guys who were too tough for filters were never allowed to play fathers. But Dwight smokes Chesterfield Regulars, not to feel tough, or not only to feel tough, but because he prefers the taste of tobacco on his lips to the non-taste of filter paper and because he likes the stronger scent of Regulars, at least for one or two cigarettes at a time. These sessions in front of the mirror, and walks down Lawrence Avenue with the Chesterfield between his fingers more often than between his lips: these are enough.

Did Raymond Cope ever wear a hat?

Taking the hat off he holds it in front of his face the way a gangster does when shielding himself from photographers.

The big mistake with Linda Dierkes was assuming she would know what his words referred to. The other mistake: settling for a routine that other people had used first, even if the people were Bogart and Bacall. He should have come up with new words. Actors can only say the lines they're given, follow the script, director, the requirements of the story. No actor can let his character wander out of the movie into a real night street where a young man walks, faking his own or the actor's toughness. But Dwight can wander anywhere. From now on he'll speak whatever words come to him. The next time he sees Judie Langerman, he will say something perfectly natural, even if he doesn't understand it himself.

Taking the Chesterfield from his mouth he gives himself a slow and very mysterious smile. Crushing out his smoke in the 1933 Chicago Exposition ashtray, stepping out to buy the week's groceries, he is again wearing the hat.

Tommy Rigney is shuffling down Lawrence Avenue when Dwight steps out of the Hi!Neighbor. The boy doesn't want to stand here with these grocery bags, surrounded by gnats in the humid evening. He doesn't want to have to figure out what to say. If he stands still, maybe Tommy won't sense him.

The man walks by. Dwight hears himself say, "Tommy."

Tommy stops, his cane swinging gently before him as if it were a metal detector. "Dwight the bright! Holy Mother of God. How's the fucking kid doing these days?"

Same old Tommy. What did his mother used to think of his language, his mother who went to Saint Bernadette every Sunday? Did she figure he had it coming, to swear all he wanted?

"Been all right. Graduate next week from Grimm."

"Hey, that's more than I ever did. And you're working, what did I hear, for the *Patriot*? Newspaper work, smart place for a kid like you. They got a good setup there, help you through college. Ma wanted Georgie to try that, years ago. Job with a future."

"Uh-huh."

"Bet your grampa's real proud of you. And your mother would have been, too. Jesus, your ma. Christ, I don't know, your ma was something."

As abruptly as he stopped, Tommy starts walking away. "Come over one of these years, we'll talk old times."

Not one of these years but one of these days he'll go see Tommy, read the comics to him as he used to do on Sunday mornings. Dwight was always the second one in the flat to wake up, ahead even of Patrice. Sunday light would be rising into the front room and Dwight would lie there imagining he could hear Marie breathing in sleep in Patrice's room. Tommy would be sitting in the kitchen with his second or third cup of coffee when Dwight came down the hall. Then the boy sat reading aloud, Dick Tracy, Rick O'Shay, Steve Canyon, Lolly, L'il Abner, Tommy's favorite Gasoline Alley, and Dwight's favorite Moon Mullins, while Tommy sipped his coffee and now and then warned the boy to keep his voice down in this flat full of sleeping people. Of black-haired Marie, asleep.

Soon then the flat came alive with a family getting ready for Saint Bernadette. Sometimes Patrice invited Dwight to come along, always he'd say No thanks. He preferred spending Sunday morning with Tommy, who hadn't been to church since coming home. Dwight recalled dimly some few Sunday mornings in a Catholic church in Centinela, Arizona; the heat in that place had been furious, as if God hated everyone there, as if Mass were meant to go on forever in that fury. So Patrice and George and Petey and Marie went off and Dwight and Tommy sat at the kitchen table eating sweet rolls and talking the Cubs.

Are these the old times Tommy wants to talk now? Dwight would rather ask him about Vera Harker. That's how Tommy knew her, Vera Harker, Vera. What did he mean, she was something. Back when Vera and Tommy were Dwight's age, what did it mean to say somebody was "something"?

He will ask Tommy when he goes over to visit, not one of these years but soon.

At seven he wakes, scratching his foot, and hears Hazard call his name quietly.

This couldn't be the end, not today of all days.

He goes in. Hazard says, "Look under the bed."

"You wouldn't josh me on my graduation day, would you?"

"Look there."

On his hands and knees the boy sneezes, and tells himself he'd better sweep out the joint again today. The old man shouldn't have to live among these dusty shapes, of mice, footballs, a bridge, a model of the Chicago *Patriot* building. Dwight emerges with a face full of dust and a flat rectangular cardboard box.

"Open it."

The shoeshine kit, product of Samuels Brush and Polish, Inc., contains a soft brush, a hard brush, three folded squares of beige cloth, a can of black polish, a can of brown polish, a tube of neutral cream. As though it were the most foreign of objects Dwight holds the kit before him. When he unscrews one can the air in the old man's room fills with the new scent of shoe polish.

Hazard says, "I won't be able to make it today after all."

"I wasn't sure if you'd have the strength."

"Well, I don't. But you'll graduate in a shined pair of shoes."

Dwight goes and gets his shoes. His grandfather watching, he kneels beside the bed and starts to work.

A bead of sweat glistens upon Richard Erie's temple as the strain of handing a diploma to each of six hundred forty-three nameless faces begins to tell. Dwight Cope, wearing well shined shoes in the Grimm High School gymnasium, reminds himself to remember the bead of sweat so he can tell the day to his grandfather exactly as it happened. But already he has managed to forget all of Erie's welcoming address, though he presumes it included the phrase, "these young leaders of tomorrow," and all but one phrase from Jerry Garth's valedictory speech: "Sorry about the air conditioning, folks, this wasn't supposed to be a remake of *Lawrence of Arabia.*" Of course Jerry would mention the movie that just won the Oscar for Best Picture; Jerry has probably never been to the Drake, never seen the kind of movies that don't get nominated for the Oscar because, as Sheffield puts it, ninety-nine percent of the people who make movies are too stupid to know a good one when they see it.

Dwight digs the heel of one shoe into the top of his other, trying to get at the bite left by whatever insect joined him in bed early this morning. He wishes Hazard could have made it here today, to appreciate the moment, early in the C's, when Erie found that the diplomas were no longer in alphabetical order and that the careful formation of the graduates had been for nothing. Since then the names have come at random, occasionally belonging to a student in the front row, more often to someone in the back who has had to push through the lines of sputtering teenagers. Now Erie's voice holds a trace of fear, though even the mothers in the crowd have stopped clicking their tongues. The principal's face has grown wider, more blank, until it reminds Dwight of nothing but a slice of Wonder Bread.

When his name is finally called and he steps forward, will the boy be recognized as the one who broke the dress code by failing to wear a belt one Monday three years ago? Summoned to the principal's office that morning, Dwight tried to explain that the pants Mrs. Rigney had given him, the ones George had outgrown, were tight enough not to need a belt. For trying to explain, he was sentenced by Erie to three days Inside Suspension. Dwight opened his mouth to ask if he had to go to

the gym and hang upside down from the high bar, and then shut
his mouth and went to begin serving his three straight days of
study hall time (two bathroom breaks and one lunch break per
day). From then on, for almost three years, he made sure to
follow the dress code. He loathed Erie too much to offer him
the satisfaction of sending him back to Inside Suspension.

A hand presses his shoulder. "Where you headed after we
stash these sweaty old caps and gowns, Dwight?"

He turns. Right behind him in the file to get out of the gym is
Jerry Garth.

"I'm headed for work."

"Listen, we missed you on the *Bobcat* this year. A few of the
staff are getting together over at my place tonight to celebrate
our hard-won freedom. Want to join us?"

"I work till midnight."

"You never know how late we might go. If it's okay with
mom and dad we might even stay up to watch the sun rise over
the lake."

Big thrill.

"Thanks anyway," Dwight says, and turns away wondering
why he said no. He should have said, Sure I'll be there, I know
the party would be nothing without me and even though you
and Judie are going steady she's secretly dying to see me. He
should have said, I'll come as a public service.

Riding the el to work he is suddenly surprised to realize it's
over. Next to last of all the graduates his name was called, and
stumbling up to grab his diploma he saw another bead of sweat
descend the temple of Richard Erie.

He should have worn the fedora to graduation. For the sake
of the fedora he had broken the dress code again last winter, the
day he made such an impression on Linda Dierkes. Then he took
to putting it on as he sauntered past Erie's office, in hope, in
fear, of getting caught. For the unpremeditated lack of a belt in

his freshman year, he had been punished; but now his intentional wearing of a hat in plain sight of the powerful went unpunished. Dwight pondered writing an editorial for the *Bobcat*: "Where is Justice?" He knew Jerry Garth would have neither the nerve nor the imagination to print such a piece.

Today, as Erie surrendered a diploma with this boy's name on it, he should have doffed his graduation cap and replaced it with the fedora.

Would anyone have noticed?

When he calls Hazard from the city room the old man says, "At least that's over with," and Dwight wonders if his grandfather is as empty of pride as he sounds. At least that's over with: as if today were the same as any other the old man has spent lying down.

"I always think better lying down." Some famous man's last words, discovered by Dwight at the Racine branch library one winter afternoon when he was supposed to be doing homework. When he went home he told these dying words to the old man and the old man laughed. James Madison. President Madison, shortest of all so far, always thought better lying down. What would make Hazard laugh now, or admit his pain? The boy could call him again and say, I know how much you wanted to be there, I know how sad you feel.

I know and I don't know.

A storm out of the Rockies is twisting through Nebraska: so Dwight reads when he rips a sheet of dirty yellow paper from the weather wire at 11:10. The wire's whirring and clicking are the only sounds in the city room, tonight being a deep yawner. The storm should hit Chicago by morning. This knowledge makes Dwight at this moment a person of immense power. A black sky is split by shocks of light, revealing a farmhouse torn apart by the storm, by his own thought. While Chicago prepares in all its ignorance for sleep a lone young man bears a vision of the city's fate approaching from across hundreds of miles of corn fields.

The party simply continues. Dwight wants to ask someone, anyone, for the time, but he wouldn't be heard over "Big Girls Don't Cry." When "Blue Velvet" comes on, the couples begin to sway to the voice of Bobby Vinton drifting through the basement. Someone turns out the lights, a girl gives a fake scream, and the song, the slow, slow dancing, simply does not stop.

He wants to stand at the center of the dance floor and announce that the storm now whirling across the plains, certain to strike town by dawn, could so easily sweep the city of Chicago into the hole in Lake Michigan. But having stationed himself against a post near one corner of the basement, he can't bring himself to move. If only he could lift his hat to wipe the sweat from his forehead, then he would be free to shout, dance, or go home, but his spine is riveted to the post, his hands trapped in his pockets, his mouth frozen in a grimace. Only his stomach is in motion, as if riding an elevator, down, down, up, down, up, down, down.

Jerry and Judie are seated on the couch near Dwight's post. He hears Jerry say: "Well, mom and dad could have sent me to Francis Parker but they felt I would develop a clearer picture of life if I went to a public school." With an immense effort Dwight is able to turn his whole body just enough to stand with his back to the couch. Still he can't make his legs move. Even while Jerry and Judie are making out on a couch a few feet away, he is stuck.

Then he hears Judie say, "Isn't that Dwight?" His head

swivels, then his legs, now all of his body is in a stiff sort of motion toward the couch. Surely he looks as if impersonating Boris Karloff in *Frankenstein*.

"Glad you could make it," Jerry says. "How's your colorful old man? Grandfather, I mean."

"Lousy," His voice cracks. He clears his throat. In a deeper voice: "Lousy."

"Dwight's got this real character for a grandfather," Jerry says.

"He's not a character," Dwight says. "I told you, remember? Last year in Spensely's class."

Jerry has gone back to admiring Judie's profile, but Judie continues listening, her attention only making Dwight feel more foolish. He doesn't mind that she's taken off her glasses, even if it is to make out with Jerry Garth. Taking off her glasses only reveals more clearly her incredibly beautiful nose. How can a nose be a thing of beauty? Dwight stands here astonished by this nose of hers, wondering if it's possible to go on having a crush on a girl while another guy is more or less breathing down her neck.

"Anyway, he's not colorful. Especially nowadays, he just lies in bed listening to the Cubs, he couldn't even get up to come today, or I guess now it was yesterday. But he gave me a shoeshine kit for graduation."

Judie says, "He what?"

"See?" Dwight pulls up his trouser legs to show off the shine, not as bright as twenty hours ago but still visible even in this dim light. As he looks down, his hat falls on his shoes. He smashes it back on his head. This time when he pulls up his trouser legs he can see his socks don't match. If Judie can also see they don't, is it possible she cares?

"Right." She leans forward to stare at the shoes and Jerry

starts kissing the back of her neck. "Ease off a sec," she says. Jerry smiles and obeys.

Judie looks up at Dwight. "You're the character."

His voice almost cracks again. "What?"

"I always said he had something going for him, didn't I?"

"Uh-huh," Jerry says, yawning.

"A real character," Judie says. "I mean, look at you: the hat, the shoes, the socks that don't match. You did that on purpose, right? I mean, you went to the trouble of shining your shoes and then wore socks that didn't match to show you didn't care, right?"

In the moments of her smile he stands speechless. This girl recognizes him as a real person, or at least as a real character, which might be even better. He could tell her how it feels to imagine himself the only person in Chicago to know about the coming storm and she'd understand. He could tell her about other stories that came in over the wire tonight, other people's lives, how they have changed in some amazing way or come to an end tonight during this party. While you were all dancing or telling jokes or making out, all these other people's lives were happening and I was the first to hear.

But she has better things to do than listen to Dwight's nonsense. For this bit of time he will just stand here in the dim basement smiling down at her while her boyfriend waits to recover her attention.

"Boy!" O'Donnell calls.

Dwight turns from the east windows and walks over. The only reporter still here tonight stares straight ahead through very small eyes while he types, as if blind or deaf or both, refusing to turn his head even when he comes to the bottom of a page, instead grabbing another set of carbons and jamming it into the typewriter without a pause. Dwight takes the sets of completed pages. Walking to Sheffield's desk he pulls the carbon sheets from each set and crumples them in his fist.

Sheffield reads O'Donnell's lead to Dwight: "For Jiri Jarosic, it was a transfer to the grave."

Jarosic, a recent immigrant from Belgrade, boarded a bus on South Halsted Street early this evening, presented his transfer, was told the transfer wasn't good on this bus, shook his head when the driver told him he had to pay, pulled out his pockets to show they were empty, became insensed when the driver told him to get off, stomped his foot and began to shout "in a foreign language the driver could not identify," shook his fist when the driver opened the front door, and was reaching into his pocket to get his wallet, which contained proof of his right to be in America, when the driver pulled an automatic from beneath his seat and shot him through the heart.

"Where was he going?" Dwight asks.

Sheffield calls out: "O'Donnell, you find out where this poor devil was headed?"

The unblinking reporter grunts.

"No," Sheffield mutters, "you wouldn't. Just the facts ma'am."

Walking around the Loop this morning, out of work, the man wandered into the Drake, to pass the time, to get out of the sun, to improve his English. In the lobby a woman struck up a conversation with him, another newcomer. She invited him to her apartment for supper, and wrote out instructions to get there by bus. Her face, her voice, were what he saw and heard the moment the bullet found its way into him.

Sheffield cuts into the boy's imagining. "Be nice to have a picture."

"Of Jarosic?"

"The driver. The face of stupidity. I always wanted to

capture the pure face of human folly. I tried once. You've seen the painting several times."

"The men bleeding—you painted that?"

"Did you think I'd spent my whole life as a night editor?"

"I don't know what you've done. You never say."

"I just said."

He speaks as if these are his last words on the subject of the past. Dwight goes to the desk opposite Sheffield's and begins typing out the "Temperatures From 'Round the World." He types slowly, waiting to be interrupted, but Sheffield is busy revising O'Donnell's article. Dwight has already reached Singapore—high 92, low 73 (even in Hobart the nights turned cooler than that)—before Sheffield speaks again, suddenly, not looking up from the page.

"I called that one 'Night Watch'. The only one I didn't destroy."

"You destroyed your paintings? You had no business doing that."

Sheffield stares at him until he decides he must have said the wrong thing. "I mean—"

The man's laugh cuts him off. "You're right, I did have no business burning those pictures. I should have let them sit around reminding me how many years I had wasted. But I imagined by burning them I could prove they were a big deal. If I could do something so dramatic to my pictures they had to be important, the burning had to be a tragedy. All it turned out was a terrible smell I left behind for Laura to deal with. Laura, my once and only. For a while she believed I had the calling. Set me up in her Lake Forest mansion and while she went off raising charity or writing for the suburban gazette or plotting to get Adlai into the White House—you see, she adored playing patron saint of lost causes—I hid out in the studio on the third floor and occasionally, as a way of drying out, actually painted.

Jesus, that was a gorgeous room, looking right out at the lake through the top branches of those oaks and red maples. Van Gogh would have given his other ear to be locked up there for life in that morning light, meals provided and a choice of warm bed: the single, right in the studio, or the double in the so-called master bedroom where I joined Laura quite often in the first year and then less and less as time limped on. Still, after six years I did have enough work to fill a small gallery, if they left a lot of tasteful blank space on the walls. She arranged a showing for me, though by this point even she must have seen the time had come to concede, a point I made more clear by turning up nicely polluted at my own opening. Nobody from her circle would have bought my work anyway, they wanted reality filtered through the homilies of the local padre. Church-of-England-one-step-removed. They wouldn't have taken the stuff for free.

"The next day I loaded every picture from the gallery into the station wagon—bought for the kids for whom she had hoped—drove to the back of the mansion and made a neat pyre in the basement. By the time the smell started rising and she came running down there I stood hosing the embers. I was careful not to set the mausoleum itself on fire, just the corpses. Then she threw me out, more or less. Six years of me were more than enough to put a decent person through."

"Boy!" O'Donnell shouts, though he could speak the word in a mild voice and be heard. The boy starts to his feet. Sheffield says, very quietly, "In a minute, O'Donnell, Chicago is not staying awake for your story."

Dwight wishes he could get the pages, go on about his work, try to make sense of all Sheffield has told him. But he has no work tonight but to listen to the man's voice. It is not a driven voice. Dwight has watched confessions in movies, where a character breaks down and spills his guts, and always the actor plays it for all it's worth. This man is doing the opposite. For all the emotion he shows, he could be reading the weather chart.

Now come the careful motions of Sheffield lighting a cigarette. The boy says, "How did the one escape?"

"That one came later." He turns in his swivel chair and points north. "I went to work for a living, something I hadn't had the misfortune to do since the war, which was definitely work though I still wonder if it qualified as living and so do a few million other people. Never mind. Damn it. Where was I?"

Turning from the window he seems troubled, not by his story but by losing his place in it.

"You went to work."

"So I did." He smiles. "A few blocks up Michigan, commercial art, the only kind of halfway human work I knew I could find right off. I still had my sketchbooks, done during the war to pass the ungodly hours of waiting, never a long enough stretch to let you unwind but long enough to drive you half-cracked. Forget that. I probably did my best work during the war, with no one watching.

"I worked hard. I dried out. Believe it or not I had this notion I'd pay Laura back for the six years. On the day I hit eighty years old, by which point she'd be going on eighty-six, I would hand over the final check and wheel back to my little pad, a free soul. The one payment I did send came back uncashed, of course. Think of the insult I was heaping on injury to this woman whose only sin was believing in me. I might have kept trying to send her the checks but soon after the first one came back I began to get very un-dry again. For a while I had worked too hard to realize how much I hated the job, the people, all the sweet banalities we employ to pass whatever time we get to spend in one another's company. These things get to you after a while if you forget not to pay attention. One Tuesday afternoon I walked out of a big meeting with a client from some textbook company, some smarmy books for defenseless kids, and went looking for an empty bar. I needed a place where I wouldn't have to listen to a word. That afternoon I still recall fondly.

Midsummer, the big plate glass window oozing light, and me in a dark corner listening to two kinds of silence, the one around me and the one in my head. You don't get too many of those drunks, the peaceful kind. When people started showing up at four-thirty I took a bottle home down Division and finished myself off there in my old apartment, another place full of light like where an artist expects to live. That evening sun filled the kitchen, and I was finished.

"They didn't fire me right off. I'm a great apologizer. To get fired I had to slip up again, which I did in short order. Then I worked a lot of places, unskilled labor, semi-skilled. Always amused me, 'semi-skilled' labor, as if one of your hands were graceful and the other clumsy. I moved from room to room, anyplace the rent left me some dough for my nourishment, which most liquor does have—all those grains. But forget that. I can't recall those days. Can't even tell you how I ended up in the art supply store but there I found myself late one winter's day. Must have been payday, I had enough on me to buy some paints, brushes, canvas. By the time I got home I had to start painting with darkness in all the windows. But here is the thing: the light never came back the whole nine days. But then not much light finds its way into my room anyway."

"You're still in the same room now?"

"After I finished it I couldn't ever bring myself to move out. Once the painting was done in that place it had to stay and so did I. Artificial light. I painted by the light of those garish lamps furnished apartments are stuck with. Chicago winter, dark from dawn to dawn. The few times I slept, I'd wake not knowing the time. Mostly I stared at the empty spaces on the canvas, trying to make them smaller. I must have drunk a few quarts of coffee but that was all. For some reason, or for no reason at all, I didn't get the shakes, the sweats, or pass out and then come to, screaming. The inside of me hurt like an empty space had replaced my stomach. Who knows how I decided the picture was done? No robin landed in the ledge by my window to let me know. I just left that one blank spot and put down my brush."

"What spot?"

"Near the top left-hand corner, behind the Prudential Building, is nothing. Empty canvas."

"That could be the lake. The hole in the world."

"No, that would have to be a blue so dark you'd mistake it for black. This is just canvas. It looks very dumb."

"Then why did you leave it?"

"Maybe I figured if I never made myself paint another I would still have this one left to finish. I don't know. Maybe I knew nothing had changed and I would never paint another stroke. Later on I bought a little box camera, took some decent photographs, then I started collecting cameras. That's how I ended up in this mighty fortress, by way of free-lance photography and some pieces I wrote on the local art scene. But no more painting.

"One thing did change. I've stayed dry for seven years. If I had made one of my resolutions I wouldn't have lasted even those first nine days. But once I had gone through the nine without noticing or even trying, I had a head start on my own self, on the shade that walks beside me offering me a shot. I took the head start and I've kept it. I don't even have to turn my head to know that shade is still here. But I'm still walking, too. And look how far I've come in seven years!"

His laugh accompanies the wide movement of his hand, a gesture that takes in the whole city room. Dwight sits there, wishing he knew what to say. What would it be like, to know "what to say" all the time, the right words for any situation? People are always catching him unawares. Last night, Judie Langerman. The night—how long ago, five years? five years ago tonight for all he knows—when Marie took his hand in the gangway, surprising him so much he kissed her. People do and say these things that leave him speechless. What should he have said to Vince Balboni when he picked the fight in the schoolyard? My father ran away and my mother got killed in a car accident. He should have told the truth, as Sheffield has told him the truth here. But how was he to know that?

"So anyway," the man says, "how does it feel to work for a once-promising artiste?

"It feels surprising."

Sheffield gets up, yawning, and walks over to O'Donnell, who actually turns his head and blinks at the sight of the night editor coming for his copy. Sheffield tears out the carbons and begins reading silently. Halfway back to the desk he stops and looks at Dwight.

"Guess what."

"What?"

"Jarosic's transfer turned out to be good."

△ △ △

July 9th

Dear Papa,

You're in luck, you only asked for one but here are three "snaps," one of the little guy on his own turf and two of the Cope family in toto. I'm glad Sissy caught Ray's grin here at Dwight tugging on my dress.

We've been in our own house more than two years now. It's not real big but fine for the three of us especially if you look at this desert as our backyard.

In case you can't tell from the pictures Dwight is pretty healthy now. I've been somewhat of a different story. Doctor Crandall has kept saying this Post-Partum Depression was perfectly understandable but after I couldn't seem to shake it he started prescribing this medication. Knowing how you feel about doctors you're probably wary, but he did come highly recommended by Lucille. He's prescribed these same pills for her when she felt blue.

Dwight is a holy or unholy terror now and then but mostly quiet and watchful. As you can see he shows more of the Cope side than Harker. If this keeps up he'll do okay.

The idea of Ray becoming co-partner is dead because Leo's partner Marv took over the whole business, which may turn out best since Ray feels happy with the mechanical side and never had much business sense. (Neither does Leo or he wouldn't have let his share get away.) As long as Raymond keeps his steady job we'll do just right.

When you say you are fine do you mean your lungs are better. You shouldn't say something and then let it go. So I'll expect to hear from you soon.

Love, Vera

September 11th

Dear Papa,

From Ray comes word I should tell you Dwight was born just in time for the start of a Cubs game. I should know better than trying to iron in the middle of the day so I came in the bedroom for a break and wrote "Papa" and then sat trying to know what should come next. In walks Raymond, home for beer and lunch in that order. Sometimes all I want's a little privacy but he seems to like to know where I am anytime, which is funny sort of since he doesn't go for my asking where he's been or headed.

Games at Wrigley Field start at one-thirty, right? So he's right. God knows when Dwight will get to see Wrigley Field. Some time not too far from now I'd like us to make a trip up there if you'd have us. This would be when Dwight's old enough to appreciate the city and all the country between here and there. Which is neither here nor there—I find myself saying that a lot nowadays. What do you think of this idea of a visit?

I'm also wondering why you wrote that one time only.

Dwight's fine now after going through mumps in July. I refuse to think about polio. No, I pray against it, which might sound funny coming from me but after what he went through right after being born if there's any justice he'll be spared worse. But then why would justice strike any child with anything?

He gets lonely sometimes, I think. Not many other families out this way yet but it won't be long now says Marv, who worked out the deal for us to buy this place.

Are you still friends with the Rigneys?

Vera

Oct. the 14th

Dear Vera,

What does your husband mean? No ballgame ever started at one-thirty in the morning, especially not at Wrigley. Now that the Series is over I can write. These years the Cubs are going noplace fast but Brooklyn meanwhile has got the best player in the Game. Who would of thought I'd follow the career of a colored? But this kid is something. Only trouble, when the Dodgers come to town half the others in the city of Chi come out to see Jackie play. I try and not pay them heed. But youd think the management would have the smarts to let them all sit with their own. Let the rest of us watch the boy in peace.

You know who asks for you? Your old friend Tommy. In fact he's the one kept after me all these years to write to you. When I'd run into him on the street. You should of seen him smile when I said you had sent me pictures of your boy.

Your pa

6.   The Return

Vera

Gone?

No because here forever pinned alone by the weight of my or call it our Chevy in the slanting afternoon light they'll find my only pain the loss of everything except the dress I made for him but we'd never met yet I knew if I made a dress to wear to the Avalon get lucky meet somebody right the first night I wore it was I ever lucky or just a dope so now they can come upon me in this funny old green almost too tight from the weight I've put on these going on six full years to end with the sun glaring off the rearview mirror into me why doesn't the sunlight hurt now at the end still I was right that night we met at Raymond Cope and me Avalon him leaning on a post at the edge of the dance floor Hawaiian shirt brighter green than my dress a real goofball to wear dark glasses inside but what did I know about him then nothing or men in general just Tommy for Sunday walks oh but what will Tommy say when he hears I and Father Wilkes will he forgive not forgive what do priests call it or Dwight what will he when he learns I

Sissy

In the morning you watch a dozen other mothers driving or walking their kids to Hillside Elementary or Saint Theresa. Sometimes the kids are crying but even that doesn't matter. And by the end of the day here comes a boy holding his mother's hand talking so hard he can barely get his breath. When his mother says, Don't talk so fast Ricky, I want to run out and say, Let him tell you his first day of school whatever way he wants.

Tomorrow won't be as hard. Second days never are.

Vera

but why feel no pain but still remember and why this cool rustling of leaves like grass but no leaves in my hearing pinned where I should feel the painful heat like usual going on six instead a cool wind I can't give a name to like the evening the two of us made Dwight in our honeymoon cabin Arrowhead Springs will Ray ever hear I don't care didn't do this to get back at him or anyone not even Hazard I know who I did it for not me either but is this Chevy mine or Ray still own half killing me in the sunlight or did he forfeit his share when he left for good Stealing's wrong I said to Dwight when he asked Where's daddy and I wanted to tell him Gone for good instead I said Finish your carrots and Stealing's wrong not forgive but what do priests call it I don't care anyway if Father Wilkes does or not or forgives my stealing the orange from McMichael's fruit stand down Wilson ran the alley some backyard porch gangway Paulina Street then our gangway to the back stairs and who had to be there but Tommy the big stupe throwing pebbles up at our kitchen window when I told him how dumb it looked for an old kid he pushed me down so the orange fell out from my dress and he said if I didn't tell him how I got it he'd push me again but when I told him I stole it he laughed saying God's gonna come and take your hands in the night and leave you bleeding stumps laughing halfscared not knowing should he believe it or not I knew I didn't and offered half the orange to his scared face later he went to confession asking Father Costello for absolution for eating half a stolen orange from a not even Catholic girl absolution there absolves but who cares if old Wilkes does me or not or if Father Costello forgave Tommy Tommy's hand what was left of thumb middle finger half his ring finger moving slow across my forehead when we took our last Sunday walk saying Go out now find yourself a man from all these millions coming back in search of a girl like you stop wasting your walks with me but I got mad saying It's not for you to say but I knew already I'd be leaving soon then the both of us started laughing there in the hot Sunday sun but here the air so cool all wrong for this air all wrong this rustling of leaves

Leo

We've got this routine. Twelve thirty-five I check in. Find out how's her day going, her's and Angela's. Then I eat my lunch but only after calling. But hardly ever any other times of day. Because if I'm calling every other hour she'll worry if I miss a time which I probably would if she started expecting it. Because you never know what will happen.

That Wednesday though, first day of school, I called a second time. Around three-fifteen. Something had caught my eye. Cruising down Comanche I saw this sign. The station was for sale. For Sale, and then the number of the company in Phoenix. No mention of Marvin Joll's name. So I called Sissy. Because it almost seemed like we had won something. I had and Ray too. Without us the station had failed. In the end Marvin was selling out. It needed the best mechanic, Ray Cope, and second best, me. Without us it was just one more crummy service station.

"Get your duff down here and I'll set you up as the best auto doctor in the Southwest," I wrote to him. Words to that effect. Summer of '45. He took my word, he came on down, the two of them. It came true except me and Ray becoming co-partners. But even that part I had believed. Thought Marvin Joll was a friend. I didn't know the man.

Sissy

Stealing is stealing. Leo can't seem to get it through his mind that what Marvin did was the same as what Leo might arrest somebody for, like shoplifting or burglary, the same as Ray stealing the Packard. The only difference, Marvin did his stealing inside the law so Leo had no recourse. But he says that made it something to shake your head in admiration at, how Marvin pulled it off legal.

But now he claims because the company wants to sell the station it means Marvin lost a bundle. But a man in Marvin Joll's position fixes it so even when he loses he wins something. There are ways we'll never know of arranging things. Can't he see that?

Then when the phone rings again around four-thirty I think, It couldn't be Leo again, he wouldn't call three times, and I'm right.

Vera

where no leaves lie and where's Dwight now scared because his mother late to pick him up and I want will they tell him all I wanted to and couldn't exactly why stealing is wrong or is it I stole Tommy's heart on our Sunday walks till I didn't know how to tell him I was running away with a stranger I'd met at the Avalon the first night I wore the green dress I'd made myself on a sewing machine bought with money that could have gone for another bond but I saved enough bonds for my son to make a start Ray's and my son a thousand in secret bonds I even borrowed from Hazard so Ray would never suspect the bonds existed how did I know from the start to save a secret part of myself Ray could never touch from the moment I laid eyes in the Avalon no all I knew right off was the way he held me when we danced only later came to me he could take me away from Hazard the factory the flat but I couldn't let him all of Why Not

Take All Of Me the first slow dance in his arms not knowing yet but soon enough to keep my one secret won't die with me in this same dress Dwight will have my thousand in the end unless God forbid Hazard makes it his own secret no my father never stole only nagged and drank and made me quit school for work but nobody makes you work unless you're a slave I could have held out and finished high school but then I wouldn't have saved my secret thousand or had to put up with the eyes of the foreman making me wish I had no body or couldn't have bought the sewing machine to make my own dress for finding a boy home from Anzio to make a son together so I could tell him Stealing's wrong and Finish your carrots Dwight just looked at me big dark eyes his father's gift asking where his daddy had gone when your kid asks you where his papa went and you know the answer is Far away forever you want to find the bastard just to kill him for making his son your son ask the question but you make yourself remember the way you felt when Ray took off his dark glasses after our first number thin scar along his cheekbone did he wear the glasses to hide the scar or call attention to it when he took them off God I wonder does he know he's good looking scar and all no not All Of Me our first slow dance wait I Got It Bad I did too and it wasn't good still got it six years later but the hell with Ray I did this for the boy we made in our cabin like Ray's mother and father made him wherever like Hazard and Alice made me her eyes in the summer night she held me when I fell in the street what made me fall hunger sickness fear of the wild streets what made the smile rise in her eyes holding me in her longarmed smell of potatoes and dirt Alice carried me home only five but must have been heavy for her me and those potatoes in her dress and my brother inside her Mama carried me home through the slaughteryard smell of the strange new summer with that smile in her eyes that she lost when the baby who would have been my

brother got born dead the light in her eyes went out then I got
too scared to move in the silent sight of her dead eyes where Pa
and I waited for her to be not that I knew what we waited for I
only knew the waiting and afraid in so much silence for one
little room waiting on her to be
gone?
no because still this rustling the way the grass will move above
me when he comes to lay me home to rest will come when the
sun dies but if gone means finding rest why did the peace go out
of her eyes when she lay close to it in the small dark room but
wait wait the peace came back to the points of light her eyes had
become the last hour coming back into rest in the same brown
sack dress she carried me home to that room later growing so
silent Pa and I took all our shoes off to ease her becoming gone

Raymond

I can fix anything, I said. The guy hired me then: come back
tomorrow ready for work. Here I am.

Raw day turned smoother now raw again. First week in
September already a cold raw day. Smart character me to hit
frozen country in September instead of March. Driving into
winter not out of it.

The right move.

Raw day's work home to a room called home. Quarter past
four. Half hour, forty minutes, then home.

This is what comes of wandering.

Still, anything, anything beats the desert. I know, I've been
around. The desert looks like hell but really is. I can take the
cold even in September. Bring on the Chryslers and Nashes and
Pontiacs that can't start for it being too cold in September. I'll
fix them.

The ones that won't start because it's too hot in January, in
Arizona? The hell with them.

Or else they're in hell already.

Sissy

I'm the one taught her to drive, and now where's she gone in the Chevy her husband left behind? Ray only promised to teach her, same as every homecoming from one of his jaunts he'd promise to stay with her forever this time. So I finally taught her in that Nash we had then. I knew she'd learn fast, her quick mind, even on those pills. Then when Ray let her know he was leaving for good by stealing a car instead of going off in the Chevy like the other times, she started taking the car on long drives, who knows where? Driving. Who knows where this time?

Mrs. Nathan is her name. "I came to pick up my Priscilla and this boy Dwight's still here where the school bus leaves them off. His mother still hasn't come. He says you might know where she is?" At the voice of a worried stranger right off I picture Vera drifting a long way to noplace in that Chevy.

"I taught his mother to drive."

Mrs. Nathan must wonder what in hell that has to do with the price of tea in China.

Vera

but mine would be a dark green with small yellow flowers not some model's handmedown from Thel's sister but green and mine with my own face dull dark blond hair not their home perm mine in the front room Pa stood watching me over the sewing machine not knowing should he be mad or glad at least I had stopped moping around and was ready to go celebrate like everyone else but still a new dress to go dancing at that place with Flo and Thelma who he just knew weren't the little girls anymore I used to play with but he didn't know if I had stopped being his little girl anymore now that I'd given up telling him to stop worrying how I spent my evenings I knew I hadn't done a thing to shame him and didn't care anymore whether he believed me or if he approved my choice of pattern or preferred

puff shoulders or Baby Doll collar instead I knew what I wanted
wouldn't even let Flo pluck my eyebrows no more of that I'll go
as I am on hot nights while all over Chicago people are out
looking for celebration there I sit our hot front room running
that machine through every flaw known to seamstresses till I
made what I wanted and tried it on for him knowing he'd never
show if he liked it instead nodded and yawned glad I'm finally
done so now he can hear his radio but I knew when I saw myself
in the wavy mirror he had brought home one night from
somebody's trash stealing is wrong but Pa never really stole like
me from the fruit stand and Pa won't steal my Dwight's
thousand but he put up this mirror so walking past the closet
door you saw yourself all wavy and puffy almost a funhouse
mirror all wrong like the toaster he'd never replace no matter
how many times broke yet even in this mirror I could tell I had
done something all my own from scratch to finish not like
working the line Lady If You Can Follow A Recipe You Can
Pack Shells and risk blowing off your hands all the shells I
packed went for others to blow off other people's heads but this
was mine I studied my work and didn't even mind the flaw I
found or care when Thel brought her sister May no June no
April who found a couple other mistakes and wouldn't let on if
she was impressed either nobody had to tell me I had done good
work how could I be here in the same dress if I hadn't made it
just right a little tight by now but why never make another all
our six years could have scrounged up a machine made all my all
Dwight's clothes too instead this the only and whatever talent
dried up bet if somebody gave me a machine now my hands
would only shake but that one time they made something maybe
Raymond the same just once tried to make a life with somebody
else and then let it go to pieces and I must have known we'd fall
away in the end so saved out bonds never knowing when he'd
come home or for how long always wishing against hope or
sense this time to stay but always keeping the thousand hidden

from Ray was a man to hold a secret safe from to know one important truth he didn't know one thousand bucks worth but the first night in my new selfmade dress I knew two things he wouldn't be long in Chicago and I would see him again oh and the third thing I knew the scar below his eye

Sissy

None of us, we're not in danger. Then why after calling Leo to ask him to drive out to Vera's and see if she's too doped up to drive or what's what, why do I go out in the yard where Angela's playing house in her box the new frigidaire came in, why bring her inside as if a storm's coming or an earthquake? The sky hasn't even started turning dark.

Leo

I hadn't made the drive in months. With Raymond gone so long. When Vera came to see us it was all right except if they stayed too long the boy got cranky and I had to hold back from hauling off and letting him have it. Not my place to discipline another man's child, even in my own house. But when we'd go out to her place I never knew what to say. If you get used to a certain person living in a place and then he doesn't anymore there gets to be a silence you don't know how to fill.

Why couldn't he have stayed with his wife and son like normal people? Once he told me the first time he laid eyes on her he started believing in fate. A dance hall this was, Chicago. Not that she was a rare beauty. He just knew it would be her or nobody. Turned to me, put down his wrench, and shook his head, saying, Now how can I believe it's fate with her and still have to keep leaving this woman for weeks or months at a stretch?

He didn't ask it like he expected an answer. Nor expecting sympathy. When I couldn't think of a word to say he picked up his wrench and went back to work.

Carburetor rebuild on a Chrysler this was.

If he didn't know the answer, how should I?

Vera

no don't give up a real home just like that I want you to think this over but when we closed our eyes on the kiss or at least I closed mine and will never know if he I saw us escaping through mountains like what'stheirnames Think it over hard I've never known a real home but you've got one here with your pop and I wondered Is this guy trying to coax me into saying yes by being sarcastic but no that made me so sad Raymond believed if you lived in one place for years with somebody that meant you had a home he imagined he was asking for a sacrifice oh how could I tell him all the ways me and Pa had nothing near a home the look in Pa's eyes whenever I did or said something he couldn't figure or how he'd always remind me it made him sick to take welfare but he had to do it for my sake but if it was only for him he'd die before taking their handouts but how could I make Raymond see any of what my life with Pa was really like I never tried it made me so sad to know he could believe Pa and I had a real home

Leo

No point breaking in, the Chevy was gone. What did Sissy think I'd find anyway? Most likely on her way home from the cafe Vera had gone off to sample the scotch at Pico Pete's or the Lazy Seven but I was damned if I'd search her down. She could come home when ready, and the boy was better off if she took her time.

Some of us just don't have it in us to wander. Raymond asked me one time how I stuck myself with a used-up woman and why I stayed stuck. He was lucky we were both too smashed to pick a fight but then he got lucky a lot in what people let him say and do. How could he call Sissy used up when she's nine years my junior? He meant she's burdened down with Angela, with all life did to the two of them. Don't you ever get the urge to leave all that weight behind? he asked me.

Some of us figure you choose one weight or another. My first thirty years, before Sissy and her daughter came along, I carried a particular kind of weight. Then I chose another. Why go back to the first?

The road west out of Hobart's tricky but with a move on I could make it to these people's house, the Nathans, pick up the boy, get back to Centinela before dark. Worse came to worst he could stay the night with us.

Raymond

Good work, the guy says. See you tomorrow. The bossman.

Why not? The next day too and the one after. Nothing but time. Money disappears by its own power, time you have to do something with or go screwy. Go screwy anyway trying. Find a room, a bottle, a magazine. Write postcards to a woman in Hellhole Arizona and tear them up. They're in hell already, me I'm a free man even if Ketchikan's nobody's notion of heaven.

Or find a tavern with not too much light or noise inside. Alibi Room. Jake's Tap. Antler Haven. This one looks better than most. Hell of a stupid name but dark enough and almost empty except for the painted brunette two-thirds of the way down the bar.

Does "Lucky to have my eyesight" work in a joint dumb enough to call itself the Silver Slipper?

One small glass of rye.

Thy Kingdom come Thy will be done Dad used to say raising the glass. On earth as it is in heaven. They left out hell.

So what if she doesn't look as sharp from one-third of the way closer? How many do? Have to get near to let her see the scar.

The rest is history or will be. Or won't, and I'll pass the evening on my own time, a free agent.

Rye, small glass.

I fix cars for a living. Hows about yourself and mine dining in style tonight? Hows if we skip the dining and move on to the style?

In the war. Not this rinkydink one they cooked up last year to take our minds off our troubles. The right war. Lucky for me it wasn't worse. I came home whole. There's a boy 3000 miles south of here proves it.

Right, a GI. Must have been, I bought a house on the GI Bill. Rye.

Vera

I want one too Raymond said and maybe he did want to try and make a home those nights after the Avalon when we couldn't go to his boarding house ladies not allowed and of course the flat was out thanks to the old man's sense of smell so we'd meet at Danny's Cafe or in the balcony at the Granville some lousy one this soldier home at Christmas starring Gene Kelly and Deanna Durbin now why remember them in that stinker but not the names of the two who flee through the mountains like I pictured us doing or once when he met me at the work bus we just walked around the Loop in the Indian Summer evening window shopping stopped for supper some decent place Hamilton's was it called he had to take one of those clip-on ties from the man but mostly we ate at Danny's where he watched me put away plates of pork chops and applesauce or stew or hot turkey sandwiches all of a sudden this appetite with him telling stories of life in an army family never living one town long enough to make real friends before torn away and now after being through the war he didn't think of them as parents not even sad but speaking a simple fact But I want a home now he said and thought he meant it but never stories of the war Lucky to have my sight I'm a lucky man he said Let's leave it at that and when he mentioned his discharge pay laughing watching me listen to him and wonder what his right move would turn out even now I can taste those pork chops like the guy in khaki trousers ate in the diner on the road to Arrowhead Springs and the ones I'd eat at Danny's are what I taste now in this last place waiting for the light to go but slowly not like for Tommy who lost the light all at once but on our Sunday walks he said he was getting used to his life now home two years Patrice and Alf didn't baby him anymore he'd found useful work sorting screws as fast by feel as others by sight and while he worked could hear the Cubs on the radio and his kid brother George read him the box scores the only thing he couldn't get used to feeling cold all the time so went around in these heavy sweaters Patrice knit him I couldn't stand the heat inside or out but Tommy got hit the minute they made the beach and lay there one whole night with the coldest water he ever felt creeping up the shore acrost his legs and then acrost his back till at dawn somebody pulled him up out free later they told him the Mediterranean where he fell was warm that time of year even at night but to him it had felt colder than Lake Michigan in March he laughed when he told me laughing more on our walks getting a little fat wanting it always warm while he told me how the light went out all at once Lucky to have my sight Raymond said Especially looking at you but when he said that I didn't even blush just looked at the yellow clock over Danny's counter six twenty-five wondering what Ray thought the right move might be and who was she to wonder this girl who sat not blushing while her looks were praised for the first time ever except when her Pa had lied to get her to quit school was she the same girl who bled into the sheets not knowing the same girl twisted in this cool light to the rustling of leaves that aren't found in the desert but I hear them just the same not yucca leaves but elm oak maple turning and lifting on a cool fall morning not this desert afternoon but Chicago autumn in a cemetery must be mine where Hazard will lay me down to rest after bringing Dwight home to live in my own room old bed where she gave her blood to the cold sheets did she grow up to eat huge suppers in Danny's in the Indian Summer of '45 with the man who had come to take her from all she had known from the flat on cold mornings before the long factory ride and endless movement of the line

Sissy

Last week she made me go with her to see that Father Wilkes. He talked of ignorant beaneaters and drunken redskins, he said things you wouldn't expect from the mouth of an old man in his position. Then he said other things you could have guessed ahead of time. The same words the Methodist preacher in Amarillo used against me when I asked him what kind of God would leave a sixteen-year-old girl abandoned with a baby like Angela who would need taking care of all her days. "A unique immortal soul . . . The ways of the creator are never clear to us in this life . . . Left to your power alone to see your child grows toward the love of God."

That's just it, Vera said, I don't even have the power to keep myself going much less see to the life and soul of a boy of five which I'm not even sure he has, a soul I mean which I hope you won't mind me saying Father but after all it was my onetime husband Ray who insisted we raise Dwight in the church (You knew which color pill she was on from the way the words spilled out of her mouth) but Ray never brought him to church himself, never being partial to Mexicans and not being around lately to take him anywhere, so it was left to me, even though I've never been a believer, but I'll tell you something Father lately I've pictured how restful it would be to believe, I want so much to believe.

Here the old man burst out laughing, saying: Restful? Are you joking? I've been believing as long as I can remember, and a priest forty-seven years, and it hasn't given me one restful moment!

I wouldn't have expected a man in his position to say such a thing.

Vera

so he did take me away the right move though we turn out wrong he turned out not a husband or father all wrong Ray us me but Father Wilkes said Nobody makes a wrong move except to turn away from God's plan all life leads somewhere even if for me it's led to ministering over the spiritual needs of a bunch of redskins and tamale-eaters then came the cold laughter of Father Wilkes or oh Tommy's high laughter when he told me his trip to confession after I stole the orange he could feel Father Costello's face screwing up in the dark box when Tommy asked would a girl get punished same as a boy A girl can be as foul a vessel of Satan as any boy Father Costello said for the Blessed Virgin herself weeps real tears over the sins of young girls when he told me this Tommy screwed up his own face laughing loud and free not like Father Wilkes choking when he told me I had it restful as I sat there at his desk where a priest talks to people face to face not confession with the sun burning through the window behind him to make me ready for dozing off except I'd swallowed a couple of Crandall's green-eyed specials before coming to see the old man so no danger of sleep and I could tell Sissy wanted to leave why did I make her come listen to the old man go on about the boy's soul in my care who waited outside the office and now here I've done this thing for his care and when the light fades it will have been done so my boy won't have to be raised by a tired halfcrazy woman but by an old man who might raise him at least halfway right and when Dwight's grown Pa will see honestly he gets my gift to start him out in life

Pa's honest and strong in his own bullheaded way but not bad he just never knew me just wanted a son and now he can have one of his own soon as this pain rises too far in me but he never could figure out his daughter take the Monday morning he came home from work to find me at the table twisted in a sob hating him for finding me like that and he must've hated me too but only gave me his puzzled look saying nothing but saying What in hell is wrong with you Vera the war is over and you're still acting stranger and stranger and crying away now for no reason at all he must have thought the strangest thing in the world ending up raising this girl who might as well have come down from the moon for all he felt like kin to her to me who could not explain it was Tommy made me cry telling me how he got blinded I went home and lay awake that whole Sunday night going over his words feeling the coldest water creep up his back while I lay there twisting the sheet in the night's heat stretching on forever why not move into the front room for whatever breeze and the radio turned low and sweet no I stayed on my damp bed his words swarming through the air through my head till I went to sit at the kitchen table letting my coffee turn cold when Pa came home to wonder who in hell his daughter must be couldn't make him feel the cold of the water Tommy felt or the wish I felt to cure Tommy's blindness with the touch of my hand to his eyelids but if you could believe in the curing of a warblind boy you could believe Crandall scrambling down this hillside hands full of beautiful colored pills Doc Crandall bringing the miracle of rest no alone no doctor no nobody coming down to me alone with Jesus this pain but everything changed when Raymond came I didn't wake up wishing to fall back asleep for good anymore nor let that goddamned foreman's eyes following my body bother me so the evening Raymond asked me to go for a ride in his brand new beatup '39 Model A I thought Well tonight's a night for chances and rolled the window down for the Indian Summer wind against my face to ride down by the edge of a deserted diamond where we parked at the edge of the beach and he switched off the motor to let us sit quiet looking out at the lake a week later we rode the Model A Chicago to Arrowhead Springs to here where that car sold to make a down payment on this Chevy which has stood us in good stead until today when the lady of the house goes and drives it off the side of the mountain but first I did everything right left the note for Hazard to give to Dwight and then the bonds when his time comes have himself a nice little start in life saw to doing all of it right and just have to wait for the finish but why not coming why this pain fade till no pain again now no feeling at all

Leo

They went to the trouble of building that road, they could at least have built something a person could drive on without taking his life into his sweaty hands. I'm surprised the insurance company insures us that far up into the hills.

When was it, Angela's birthday? Last March, not long before Ray pulled his Grand Theft Auto, his grand farewell. They had us over for a birthday party, three of us and the three of them. Vera baked a cake. I told Ray to look into buying some insurance. Not that it meant a thing to me, Gary Huff's not about to hand me a cut of his commission. But no family should get left out in the middle of nowhere. You never know what could happen.

But then there's no such thing as Desertion Insurance, is there?

Whoever heard of somebody coming and stealing a car in broad daylight from a repair shop? That's how Ray pulled it off. He knew the running of the place from the years we worked there, the years it was our place. And he was too unexpected. But imagine when Marvin heard his former employee had swiped a Packard from the shop Marvin now owned. Imagine Marvin Joll explaining to the owner of the Packard.

That high on the road you can't see back down to the desert floor, just rocks and steep drops. Hell of a road. Anybody not careful watching can skid right down just like that. I was driving so slow I saw the skid marks.

Vera
the only feeling his hands on my legs fine Raymond's hands fine on my thighs I would have gone on though this was the way I had never wanted it some kind of scared fumbling in the back seat still I'd have let it be that way with him but he stopped and looked nervous like the first night at the Avalon when he took off his sunglasses but this time he turned away to look out at the lake saying Arizona saying I'm going to find a place of my own land of my own home you've got a real one here think this over careful Vera because I'm no bargain and I don't mean this scar under my eye I mean I don't happen to get along much with people so you better think hard Vera Raymond made me smile the way he said Don't happen to get along but it wouldn't matter how he said any of it or how long he wanted me to think it over I could have thought all night and come out with the same word only three weeks had passed since they played I Got It Bad at the Avalon and out on Lake Michigan a tanker moved smaller and smaller into the dark Wait till that ship's gone from sight before you give an answer so I half closed my eyes and when I couldn't see the tanker I said Next Wednesday I get paid next Wednesday night we can leave then he opened up a pint for the two of us to seal our engagement with a gulp of rye the ship gone then even when I strained my eyes for it we kissed and when I opened my eyes a yellow sky hung over the lake and a desert when we kissed again would the lake have felt warm if we'd gone swimming after I said Yes making up my mind then

there to tell nobody not Flo or Thelma not even Tommy because
loose lips sink but Tommy found out later the Mediterranean
warm that time of year on the North African shore where he lay
one night and where would I be now if not for saying Yes to Ray
not crumpled here in my moment and where Dwight as Father
Wilkes said Where would your son be if you had not made the
choice you made and come to this place yes this land of its own
beauty grows on you over the going on six years reaching me
slowly till now I can't imagine living again in the chill through
my ankles dark mornings learning to make myself walk
barefoot to give the old man his last moments of sleep these
desert afternoons all I can want now but soon going back to
Chicago where the fall morning leaves he lays me down in but
why didn't I ever use these endless days of light to get me
through my bad times here instead of leaning on Crandall's
magic pills of a bum doc hooking me till even Ray told me Stop
taking them though he wanted me on them in the first place
when my Post-Partums wouldn't leave me be Ray said Go
ahead take them if they'll make you be your normal self again
but not to blame Ray my decision and kept making the wrong
one till tempted to use Dwight's bond money for more thank
God if there's one to thank for never using his bonds to feed my
own dumb craziness but why in this hell of my own making did I
believe Lucille when she said No problem use the reds to come
down from the greens as long as you stay away from the scotch
at the same time or any other liquid sustainer including Pa's old
favorite rye kept in his secret bottle did he think I'd lamp him
for a drunkard but no drunkard stays on any job long as that man
or has got the kind of strength I can't put a name to but it's there
in him but not in me or Ray for that matter though God
Raymond can get sweet take the morning he drove home too
early for lunch saying Forget lunch let's go for a drive hell let's
drive to Phoenix so we dropped Dwight with Sissy and went on

our own way which turned out to be merry all the way down to a Phoenix jeweler You've got the prettiest earlobes any woman west of the Mississippi he had told me once maybe not the most endearing words a woman ever heard but when he showed me the earrings he had picked out for me I didn't mind each one a tiny leaf in gold if only I hadn't lost the one and then thrown the other out after he left this last and final time I could have worn them today for what they'd be worth on me now instead just these pretty but bare earlobes and a low roar in my ears that could be the Chevy in its ending moments or the music box I brought along to play while I drove over the side but God knows how far the music box flew when the Chevy flipped and flipped again or could be what you really hear when you pick up a seashell not the ocean but your own heart beating

Leo

The marks, and the bush that she must have flattened.
I pulled off. I set the handbrake.

Raymond

Catch as Ketchikan. Have to know a town better than I know this one to get the best of it. Meanwhile make do with what comes to you. This one here doesn't say much and even if that's her only plus it's a big one. Can't take when a woman talks right in the middle of it. Now and then Vera used to. Telling me her love and how I made her feel. Distracting. But then came times I'd want to hear her tell me we wouldn't always be stuck in that desert, there was a life elsewhere. Then, nothing. Silent, or else telling me she forgives me running out on her and knows I won't again.

Where did she come off thinking she knew? I must have kept doing it to prove her wrong. No other cause for a man with wife and son to commit such escapes. She was my wife too even if I thought of her more as Vera Harker than my own name. The boy is just plain Dwight and the way Leo and Sissy and Vera herself used to go on about him he'll make his way in the world. Even with some of my features he must have little enough else in common with his father. All the better for him. I used to freeze up around him like there was something he wanted from me I'd never offer or be able to. In that place there wasn't much to give a kid but wind and heat, heat and wind.

If it was hell why did we move there? Why stay such years?

This one's so wordless she makes me want to say something. Almost.

Over and done. Lucky for her I didn't spill out the story of my life. Lucky for both of us. Start sounding like my ex. Better this way. Not a thing to ask for or deny but a dose of amnesia.

Vera

but if my heart's still with me then shouldn't I be on fire with thirst instead only a tickling where thirst ought to be no water before Communion Father Wilkes told me trying to get me to join up last week You belong in this church more than most of my parishioners it's not enough I buy their clumsy handmade cards to send every Christmas to Pa the Rigneys the Reeses the DeMaestris and even Marv and Lucille who I'd rather see dead than having a Merry but Father Wilkes wants me an honestoGod child of Rome but a vessel of Satan must be more pure than the Blessed herself wait Father Costello said such words to Tommy or lies to that effect but here I am anyway not taking Communion but would Wilkes approve since I took no food or drink since midnight of course he wouldn't not suicide Last Refusal of the Damned or whatever he called it last week could he tell what I had in mind his face as blank as Fat Walter the Shoemaker's the day I stuck out my tongue at him but if Wilkes here would he give me my last nights rights or Extreme Whatdoyoucallthem or would he turn me over to Crandall as

an unabsolved unsolved heathen but at least I did one of the
sacraments Father does marriage count even if you get it done
by a Justice no I guess we should have done it proper but we
wanted it over with how come I remember the witnesses the
almost deaf old woman's words beforehand to dumb Malcolm
but can't remember the wedding itself except the stripes of
sunlight through the blinds and poor Raymond almost dropping
the bolt of gold he's bought at a pawnshop and Malcolm
grinning at the near fall of the ring until it's done now we're
changed I can kiss my husband's taste of sweat and Life Savers
did something change inside when the Justice said I now
pronounce you no but when I close my eyes on our kiss I don't
see Pa anymore instead Alice carrying me home in her smell of
potatoes ammonia old sack dress and a different sweat than the
sweat Raymond smells of or this my dying here in blood and
twisted metal shock of pain through my chest let it die let me
fade away easy like smoke like evening light let fade the stunned
hurt in my cheek jaw eye when Ray let me have it I'd forgotten
you get to see stars if hit hard enough the stars turned in the
turning room like when Hazard then I saw Dwight saw the
bottle in Ray's hand if I could talk at that moment I'd cry out
Don't let your son see you smash that bottle in my face but must
have passed out a second because then the bottle was all smashed
on the table not on my face and Ray stood over me quiet and
frozen hands blotting out his own face Dwight noplace to be
seen must have run back out to the desert floor like he said at
Angela's birthday I want to sleep out on the desert floor we
laughed and laughed then all but Ray saying The Kid's not as
funny as you make out poor Ray his son made him nervous right
from the start stuck in his fear of a helpless thing counting on
him to come through year after year this thing he'd made but
didn't want his home so he had to keep breaking out longer and

longer times crashing out like Humphrey Bogart dies so Ida
Lupino can say he crashed out till finally Dwight doesn't know
his own dad who couldn't stand when others thought his kid was
funny Ray'd get antsy or get mad though I never saw him hit the
kid left the spanking to me and the answering take the morning
Dwight grabbed the Cherrios box What's that word mommy I
told him Free a little car free inside How do you spell free he
said while I'm digging around the Cherrios trying to grab that
car Dwight's asking How do you spell free till it hits me the
kid's not even five yet and here he asks how to spell this word
and I grab him so sudden I scare him but I had to hug him for
asking that question just for one long second hold him close

Leo

I could see what was left of the car, but not her. By the time
I'd be able to get down that far, if I could even get down
without ropes and such, it would be dark. But by the time help
arrived it would be dark anyway. So after calling in for an
ambulance I strapped my flashlight to my belt, crouched by the
flattened bush, let myself start crawling down. I wanted it to be
me reached her first. Not some stranger.

Sissy

I can put the meatloaf back in the oven for whenever Leo gets
home, Leo and Dwight if it turns out that way, but I can't make
Angela wait any longer. Serve her supper and I'll take my mind
off the phone.

"Remember Daddy's and my wedding day, Ang'?"

She nods. What does she think about before nodding? What
pictures pass through her mind?

"Auntie Vera took our picture, remember? The one on the
bureau. See?"

"Yeah," she says with this big sigh, the most patient girl in the world to sit through her mother's rambling.

"Now their wedding was different, her's and Uncle Raymond's."

"You told me." She drops a third of the stick of butter on her potatoes.

"Too much, Ang'. How many times do I have to tell you?"

"You told me."

And while I'm spreading some of her butter on her bread, I tell her again.

"The Justice of the Peace was bald, bald but young. Auntie Vera thought that was funny. And the witnesses were an old lady and this tall blond-haired G.I. Maybe it looked more official to have a soldier for one of the witnesses. There was some mixup, the Justice couldn't find the form right away, so while they're waiting the old lady turns to Vera: 'Me and Malcolm make a fine pair of witnesses. I can see perfect but don't hear so good anymore and Malcolm don't speak but his hearing's dandy, so if anyone wants to know I can swear out loud I saw you two get married and Malcolm can write down he saw it happen and heard it too.' Of course Vera wondered how Malcolm had become a soldier if he couldn't talk, or maybe he'd lost the power of speech along the way. But it wasn't the sort of question she could ask a stranger on her wedding day.

"Now I never told you all that before, did I, honey?"

She shakes her head.

Vera

right then I knew I would teach him to read so whenever not working or drinking or sleeping off the drink or the pills I've taught my son till he can read and write words like Free Train Dog and his name last week he wrote DADY till Sissy showed

him how and then he wrote TREE DADDY HOUSE SUN
DADDY HOUSE DADDY when I picked him up he gave me
the page folded up like a gift and while he slept that night I sat in
the kitchen looking out the window at nothing at my own self in
the bare light finishing off a bottle of port wondering where in
the U.S. or Mexico his wayward father might be at this moment
or was he studying the sights of Canada this time that far in
eight months gone one two three thousand miles from the only
sound my own breathing or the desert wind while I stared at
Dwight's words awaiting sunup or nothing wishing Ray dead so
he'd never know what a son he had fathered but how would I
know if he was dead right now or if alive how'd I know where
or how far from me teaching words to a kid who counted on me
alone to come through keep bringing home bread and love to
this home in the middle of nowhere any man hung his hat
anymore yes the port put me in a fine state by sunup when
Dwight came out asking why was I up so early I couldn't get a
word out for fear I'd burst out shouting or crying in a weary
sorrow he'd never understand but when he started writing
words again on that page I ripped it out from under his pencil
my fists tearing it apart No more Dwight in a voice so trapped I
didn't know it was mine No more writing those words but then
he had to go and grab the torn pieces from my fists till I slapped
his face hard and again and as I wait once more hard and as I pull
him scrawny into my arms holding him in the waiting for his
wind to return so he can start wailing instead of that awful
soundless sob they make when they can't breathe out their pain
and shock I know I can't carry on in this moment of holding him
know I can't be a mother to this boy anymore another ten days
much less years at Sammy's or wherever I might find another
job after pills and booze get me fired not this broken soul and
from then on it all began to come more clear and from then on

I've seen it on and off with an almost perfect brightness living the same life not a hint to anybody right up through this morning when I wrote last words to Dwight for Pa to find and counted out the bonds a brightness clear up to this afternoon turning the steering wheel just that little to send me over the brightness has led me on but even now so many things dark again like what keeps Leo and Sissy going the knowledge they've got each other not one alone but why not enough for me and Raymond and what would Ray have done if ours had turned out like Angela would he have run out for good that much sooner oh there's so much to make you ache with rage so much dark and darker still winter dawns on Paulina turning coldest in the time it took to walk barefoot across the kitchen and start the coffee and how come I never got my diploma after we came down here we agreed I should or never made another dress these six years or take the way I remember some dumb things like the old lady's words of witness who saw just fine but didn't hear so good anymore Angela's birthday face when she bit in turning into one grin of surprise as though she'd forgotten what chocolate tasted like Ray's hands like cold gloves when we walked through Lincoln Park our first date after the Avalon I didn't mind his hands didn't mind the sulphur smell we found when we drove out to the cabins edge of Arrowhead Springs best honeymoon accomodations in the county the Justice said but we found a smell of ten thousand matches getting blown out all at one time Ray laughing Hell we used to pass through places when I was a kid Hot Springs Sulphur Springs in Colorado Kentucky California but never thought I'd spend my wedding night in one Me neither I thought but didn't mind only wanted into the damp dark cabin where the double bed stood beneath the clouded window and we could hear the shouts of kids in the woods out back the same sound we woke to the next morning children in the woods behind our cabin

Raymond

Meant to buy a clock today. Another night without, count on my stomach to wake me in time for work. No way of telling how long I dozed, long enough to let her make a getaway. Rifled through my trousers most likely, the bureau and what all else in search of a sawbuck. No such luck, come back payday sweetheart.

Dreamed a stairway made of wood and fenders, at the end of it a man who looked and sounded like Dad but he was supposed to be Vera's, whose name escapes me. Harker, Harker, Mister Harker. Never had the pleasure but here he stood raising me a drink with the words Thy Will Be Done like Dad used to. But this was hers and I knew better than swallow whatever brand of poison his glass held. Then his face changed to my own saying, Son so long as we're apart may you be well.

Dreams can kill you. If only you knew where they belonged they'd have no hold, but who can say? Open a bottle and forget them but that can kill you too. Go down the street instead and put some solid food into myself. Sleep till my insides tell me it's work time again, work time tomorrow, work time the next day, next day, next day.

Whatever else tomorrow remember a clock. Whatever else find some postcards, pictures and a roll of tape. Come back up here and stick the pictures on these walls.

Any room can use a little fixup. A little color.

Vera

but when we first come into the cabin suddenly Raymond says Hell I forgot you know to carry you across the threshold but instead of us stepping back out so we could enter right he sits on the edge of the bed resting his face in his hands Ray I say Ray what's the matter and move beside him his damp hair sticking to his forehead words going straight into his hands oh it felt bad to see him there no light into his eyes so I touch his hands with mine and he looks up saying Too much moving we get to our new place I swear I won't get the urge again and then after that we lie down together on this lumpy bed where through the window I can see the sky going silver to the east his hands fast and rough at my blouse my hands slow acrost his back wanting him to slow down more than anything wanted this one moment to keep on and did my eyes hold the smile came into Alice's eyes when she picked me up in the summer evening street smile her eyes held till my baby brother slid into life without life where she lay breathing like the long whistle of leaves I can't hear anymore eyes no strength where you could rest they hadn't turned to points of light yet the peace hadn't found them yet peace of God this of my God pain wait this searing into crushed into this womb of my self killing the Chicago leavesound that were never here flooding sun into me waves of poison light if only Crandall now at last down this hillside welcome his sad smile small hands I used to lie reading wonderful names on the bottles waiting for spark of life to take me but this too much worse now to wait for him shock of twisted nerves crying where's the peace supposed to come over me now release into rest or knowing the end of knowing that something happened back there in that cabin and before his grandfather came to raise him I took him out to this hillside where he asked me to name every wildflower and still I don't know their names yet he grows one instant closer to his new life with Pa but how fast do you grow at age five Mama would know she held me at five carried me beyond the shock of another wave and does the pain fade or she could tell me if this is gone?

or will she come tell me true to free me from this burning inside me Tell me true like used to say if I told a fib Tell me true you'd say

or this?

still say to Dwight Tell me true and then he comes out with it like I did when you'd say Tell me true or carried me home in brown sack dress won't you tell me now the word to take me from here now in your dress of brown eyes light smile long arms folding me into you

Dear Papa,

This time at least it rained and I pretended the rain was snow so it would seem like the Thanksgiving when a blizzard shut down school the day before. Chicago's earliest blizzard they said. Remember? Sixth grade I must have been, Thel and Flo and I played in the street all day, Mrs. Reese made split-pea soup for the bunch of us and the best was knowing no school the next day or all the way till Monday. And the next day was white too, a white Thanksgiving.

Remember? Back when I hated school.

I shouldn't complain about the sunshine here. Nobody should complain. This weather will work wonders on your lungs. I know. Come visit, I promise it will.

Leo and Raymond tried to outdo each other in the bottle department which wasn't what made it a Thanksgiving to remember. Sissy and Angela and me, we enjoyed our own good time. Sissy had Angela back at the start of the war, in Texas this was. She's seven now but they wouldn't know what to do with her in school so she stays home. Ray says Leo did a hell of a number sticking himself with a usedup woman and her dope of an illegitimate kid. Far as I can tell they're happy enough.

Being grown up feels strange sometimes.

I miss Lucille, they all moved this fall to Scottsdale, I think I told you they were moving? Marv made a big killing with some land and decided Scottsdale would be the next place to as he put it explode. Lucille was a friend but I learned early on to stop trusting Marv. Leo didn't learn till too late and now he says he's got to admire the way Marv cheated him legal. The upshot, Ray doesn't work for Leo anymore, he now works technically for Marv, who called from Phoenix and told Leo that Ray's "general irresponsibility will have to be curbed." Leo passed these words along to Ray over turkey and trimmings, of course he grinned when he said it. Ray laughed his little laugh saying maybe Mister Marvin Joll Senior doesn't realize he's got the best car doctor in the Southwest on his payroll.

Which Ray is, the best. Sometimes he even goes as far away as Boyerton to work on people's machines. It's almost like he doesn't want to fix them exactly right because then he won't ever see them again. Some days he can only talk about whatever car he's been working on. Other times he can take the job or leave it.

I could tell you some stories about Dwight but Lucille used to do that about Josie and Marvin Junior. Mothers must think every little thing their kid does is the living end. (What do you mean, one-thirty in the morning? Dwight came in the afternoon, same as the telegram said.)

Give my best to Tommy and his folks. Whenever I'd go see Tommy Patrice made a point of asking after you. Did I used to tell you?

Love, Vera

Pa,

Here's the first Christmas card I ever sent you.

Vera

7. Other People's Lives (2)

Waiting in the right-field bleachers for the game to begin Dwight wonders if coming out to Wrigley Field with one thousand eighty-nine dollars in his pockets might have been a mistake. In the moment Pat Piper calls "Play ball!" something else occurs to him: he could have spared three bucks for a box seat today, could have gone and sat for the first time in his life among the people of wealth and seen the players for the supermen they are. Instead he walked the extra block to the bleachers, as if he were not himself a wealthy man or as if his wealth had to be hoarded for some unknown purpose. Sitting here on the usual bench of peeling green paint, watching the players go about their slow business, Dwight remains unconvinced of his new ownership. Without a notion of how he'll use the money in his pockets, he can't believe it belongs to him. All he owns now is the fear that he will spend it on small things before the big, secret, purposeful thing reveals itself.

If Hazard had given some explanation this morning, maybe the money would make sense. But the old man said, "Your ma saved these for your high school graduation," and then said nothing while Dwight stood staring at the contents of the torn yellow envelope, studying how his mother's name and his own were typed on the same line on some of the bonds and on two separate lines on others. When he turned to go his grandfather spoke again: "I should've handed these over yesterday, but I didn't want to snow you under too many gifts at once."

161

"That was real thoughtful."

"Yep. And maybe this'll shut up all your sassing and griping."

The game drags on, the crowd silent or surly. In the heavy light the boy examines his shoes. Before heading to the bank this morning, he shined them again. Now he decides a shine can only do so much for this pair. He'll need new shoes if he's going to start looking his best.

His laughter at the thought of himself in rich man's shoes is drowned by the catcalls of the fans at the Mets' right-fielder Rod Kanehl falling flat on his face in pursuit of a fly ball. The boy jumps up, ready to leap into the damp outfield, run to Kanehl, and hand him all the money: "Here, you made it to the big leagues."

"Down in front," a woman shouts: Olive Pennell, written up every couple of years in the paper, claims to have sat in these bleachers for every single home game since '32, the year Babe Ruth called his shot here. What is Dwight, a man of substance, doing here being shouted at by Olive Pennell when he should be driving the country in search of the Girl in White? After she left him behind he tried taking her place at the diner but he couldn't stick with it, small town life wasn't really for him. So he came back to Chicago hoping it might feel like home again. Now he knows better. It's time to hop another Greyhound or put some of his newfound wealth into a used BelAir convertible and go looking for her.

This coming Saturday, when he meets Sheffield at the Drake, he'll tell him the new ending.

"Down in front, I said!"

Dwight turns and bolts up the stairway, past Olive's gold and purple hair and the few other suffering fans, not stopping till he reaches the fence and can look down on the street and up at the giant Baby Ruth sign atop the apartment building across the street. All the money in his pockets could not make the beer man believe he is twenty-one. When he told the bank teller this morning that he wanted to take all his mother's bond money in cash, her eyes took on a plaintive expression that put him in mind of Joan Fontaine. In the end he let her talk him into leaving one hundred behind in savings. Otherwise he'd now have $1,189 on hand, which would still not be enough to convince the beer man. But if he pulled out all these bills, pushed his fists through the diamond-shaped openings in the fence, and let go? In the past half-hour the wind has shifted, the money would blow right back into the stands, people would be too busy scrambling for those twenties and fifties to notice a strange skinny kid walking away empty-handed and smiling. If only Sheffield could be here to see it. But Sheffield won't come to a ballgame. Who then? The old man would not get the joke. If the old man had the strength to come to Wrigley Field he'd have the strength to strangle his grandson for such an act of infamy.

Your mother left these. He opens his eyes, his hands are empty, the money nowhere, he turns, the crowd sits quietly. When he jams his hands back into his pockets the feel of the money lets him exhale. He smells his palms, sweat and old money, your mother left these. Here now? She never came to this place. Her father never brought her here. What would she have made of all this waiting and watching? He clenches his eyes shut, knowing she won't come and take part in this recreation, this dull hum. He does not feel her with him here in the breeze off the lake.

Turning to go he bumps into a man carrying a full cup of beer in each hand. One cup tips, Dwight and the man stand watching foam and beer slide out on the catwalk. "Holy criminy," the man says, "you better—" but Dwight has pulled a ten-dollar bill from his pocket and dropped it at the man's feet. He walks away without waiting to see the bill fall into the spreading pool. "What is this?" he hears the man shout, and walking faster into the cool darkness beneath the center-field bleachers he cuts into the Men's Room.

As if expecting to see his grandfather on all fours, he stops. Not even the stain remains. The boy stands at the spot where Hazard crouched. No trace.

When he walks out of the Men's Room he doesn't turn to look at the field but continues down the ramp even though the whole way he can hear the crowd behind and above him, waiting for an end.

"Hell and Creation, what are you thinking of?"

Late for work on his seventeenth birthday Dwight stands at the foot of his grandfather's bed, listening, playing with his windbreaker zipper while the old man tries to sit up.

"I handed you the bonds Wednesday. You've been walking the streets three days with a thousand bucks in your pocket. Don't tell me, a thousand plus interest. All you had to do was leave it there. The godforsaken money in the godforsaken bank where . . ." His voice gives out.

" I know it's the dumbest thing," Dwight says. "But I need the money with me wherever I go or else something's missing. Crazy. But if I knew what to do with the money I could go ahead and that would be that."

"Do with it?" The old man whispers. "Put it into the future."

"I've said it twenty times, Grampa, college is for people who can make something of themselves. Anyway, you quit school in the seventh grade."

"Look how far I went. In the ground for nineteen years, then kicked back out with a dead pair of windbags."

"But you always said that's the way of things. You even made my mother quit school."

"Who told you that?"

"What do you mean, who told me? You told me." The boy sees Hazard's face as it looked four years ago, fuller, the eyes more clear. The day before Dwight's first day at Grimm High the old man handed him money for school supplies and said, Don't expect more where that came from and don't assume I'll treat you any different from how I treated your mother. Suits me, Dwight said, the law says I have to finish but I don't care. The old man shook his head: Son, in this house I'm the law, if you finish or don't finish it's up to me. This isn't a house, Dwight said, This is an apartment.

Even today he wonders why the old man didn't hit him when he said that. Wonders why he has never hit him once in their going-on twelve years together.

"Maybe you're the one should have quit," Hazard says. "You took less from it than she would have."

"You mean you're sorry you made her give it up?"

He waits. The old man lies silent.

"She was smart, wasn't she? My mother was a smart woman."

"What do you know? You were five."

"I know how old I was. Why do you think I'm asking you? I just want a few little things out of all you remember, to add to the little I remember. Tommy Rigney told me she was 'something'. What did he mean by that?"

"Ask Tommy."

Dwight zips up his windbreaker. "I'm late." He goes down the hall, out the front door, but his grandfather's words follow him out.

"She taught you to read."

The kid wants me to tell him who his mother was, or something. How should I know that answer? If I'd give him the letters they might tell him what she went and did to herself, where she was headed. No point giving him that one more burden. Let him go on believing in accidents.

If only he didn't ask questions about her. Back around twelve, thirteen, he never raised the questions I expected. About the world, the way of things. Either they covered that in school or he picked it up from his pals. Or never learned a thing but felt too embarrassed to come to me. But now always asking after his mother. Long past the age when I thought he'd plague me with questions.

The waitress, who is not young, does not have jet-black hair, who, above all, snaps her gum while taking Dwight's order: this waitress shouts the order into the kitchen in a voice so devoid of mystery Dwight checks the other people at the counter to see if anyone else might have noticed. These people go on eating their late lunches or early suppers.

Sheffield is one whole movie and a set of Coming Attractions and half of another movie late. Why should Dwight care? People have other lives, other people have lives of their own. Sheffield, too; nobody could be as alone as Dwight imagines him. Fine. Let him have a life.

The boy's fingers tap out the time till his pie and coffee will arrive.

"Were we supposed to meet for the one-thirty show?"

He smells liquor on the breath before he realizes to whom the voice belongs. He has never heard Sheffield so careful of his diction. As if ashamed of himself, the boy looks away. "Let's grab a booth," the man says.

Dwight follows him to the window facing Clark Street, facing one more hot Sunday in front of the Brass Penny, an empty bus blocking the view of the Drake marquee. The bus waits, both doors open. Can you say a bus is hungry? What do you call it when you give life to an object? Persona something.

A soul. *Persona non grata*. No. Something else. The soul of the CTA bus at the corner of Clark and Monroe on a Sunday afternoon.

"You're mad," Sheffield says. "I stood you up."

"That's your business." He can feel the man looking at him.

"So tell me, were they great movies? Make your list of the top thirteen of all time?" His diction is unbearably perfect.

Dwight shakes his head. "I walked out on the second one. All that Biblical stuff, you know, I can only take so much of people stomping around in tents and then twenty thousand Arabs getting together and hacking at one another with swords."

"Most of those Arabs are played by Jews. Sometimes by Italians, if the movie's really cheap. Mostly Jews, like those Jewish Indians John Wayne is always coming up against. In the biblical movies they cast Jews because they make everything more comical. These are the people who wrote the Old Testament, for God's sake, if not for them Victor Mature would have made his living posing for bodybuilding ads. He's not Jewish himself, of course, the leading roles in these movies never go to Jews, just the secondarys and extras. Edward G. Robinson in *The Ten Commandments*."

"How could Robinson be a Jewish name?"

"Emanuel Goldenberg," says Sheffield. "Born in Bucharest. His ancestors put The Book together. Hollywood's the logical outcome, Jews casting other Jews to make secret jokes on the Bible. Anyway, I'm sorry. We had a date and I screwed up."

The waitress pushes the slab of pie and cup of coffee in front of Dwight. "Next time tell me when you decide to take a walk." After she walks away, he figures out what she's talking about. "Sorry!" he calls, but she has disappeared again. He tastes his banana cream pie, which turns out to be pineapple cream, and wishes he hadn't apologized.

"You screwed up all right," he says.

"Which is why I apologized. These things happen."

"What things?"

Still afraid to look at Sheffield's eyes, Dwight looks past him at the hats on the rack, men's hats, women's hats, on a day as stifling as this. Sheffield says, "Someone has a fall every minute of the world. We make a new monster, the only creation we can call our own, it reaches inside us and wrenches our guts around. Let's talk about something else. Happy Day-After-Your-Birthday. Tell me what you got."

"A shoeshine kit. For graduation, that was. And some money from bonds my mother left behind. I'm carrying it right now."

Sheffield strikes a match and watches it burn down. "You're carrying that money around? Are you trying to be a bigger fool than me?"

"Why not? I need an ambition in life."

"I've got a better one for you." He lets the flame burn all the way down to his fingertips before pressing it out. "Find your father."

"You must have had one too many."

"I did. One day at age fourteen I stole a shot from a bottle of scotch my mother kept hidden under the kitchen sink. The only shot I ever needed. But listen to my idea. You talk about your mother more than your father, but he's the one who might still be alive. She's dead."

"So I've been told."

"You mean you don't believe it?"

Dwight shrugs. "No, I just mean I don't remember any of that, the old man coming to get me or anything. I do recall the train ride, not a picture in my mind but a rhythm in my chest if I sit and try to bring it back. But the rest of it, no. I don't remember her dying anymore than I remember my father driving off in a stolen '49 Packard."

"So you don't know which way he headed?"

"West, I assume, northwest. California, Vegas."

"Fine. Start out in the paradise where you were born, and head northwest. You'll never find him, and if you do you won't know him, so don't set out hoping for some dramatic reunion. The idea is to have a reason to keep moving, a trail. You're a rich man now, you could cover a few thousand miles before your stake runs out, and then you've got a genuine skill—you can cook a few items and can learn a few more. You're employable. Go do it. You'll never find him but think what you will find in the meantime."

To Dwight's surprise the waitress has come over with a cup of coffee for Sheffield. He must have made some sign when Dwight was looking elsewhere. "Don't be a stranger," Sheffield says as she walks away. Maybe adults spend their lives giving out secret or half-hidden signs; some get through, most don't. Or did Sheffield simply mean he'll want more coffee soon?

"He'll be in a hotel with ROOMS FOR MEN FIFTY CENTS A NIGHT on the side, like the Wilson—"

"Wait," Dwight says, "you said I'd never find him."

"—staying on the seventh floor. The elevator's busted so you walk up the cold flights. A small town in Idaho, North Dakota, you got off the train just before the blizzard hit and now blue snow has begun to come down as you start up those seven flights. Rickety stairs, one continuous draft, and on every landing a slab of window to look out at the town turning blue. When you reach his door you feel inside your coat for the gun."

"What gun? I'm not going to—"

"No, but you come there ready for anything. The door's open, and there he lies on the sagging bed in his work pants and dago T-shirt."

"He was no dago."

"Lots of men wear dago T-shirts. Without stirring, he says,

Come on in kid, I just finished unpacking. You look around. This twelve-by-fifteen room is full of his life. Pieces of metal, shoeboxes of screws, bolts, wing nuts, tiny wrenches. One large suitcase lies open to reveal the guts of an engine, another shoebox has been filled with useless hundreds of bits of wire, a paper bag holds two dashboard radios. Also useless are the cracked headlights lined up against the wall, the amputated door handles scattered around the foot of the bed. You stand there dizzy with the smell and touch of all this metal. Next to him on the bed is a fat canvas bag, inside are hundreds of keys, some labeled, most of them blank. His hand reaches in and explores these keys like the hand of a blind man.

"The windows shiver. Leave me the gun, he says. But you want him to find his own way of putting life behind him. You drop the gun in an alley, where someone will find it next spring, and you go see how to get out of town in this blizzard. You've seen enough bus stations and roadside cafes, you've seen enough of your father."

"I'd come back to Chicago then," Dwight says. "Broke and all, come back and start over finding an ambition."

Sheffield crushes his smoke and takes out another. He's really smoking now, not pretending to. "Maybe you could get a woman to keep you."

"Keep me. What's that?"

"What my wife did for me, sort of, only when you're kept you're not married, at least not usually, and you don't earn your keep by painting pictures. Would you like that?"

Dwight shakes his head. "You don't have to make fun of me. I know I'm a chump when it comes to girls. To women."

"Define a chump-when-it-comes-to-women."

"He covers his walls with pictures of movie stars from twenty years ago and can't say a word to a real girl. Last week Judie Langerman started talking to me at this party, and once it hit me she didn't think I was some bug crawling around the floor, from that point on I couldn't speak. Meantime, half the guys at Grimm High are getting somewhere with half the girls I ever looked at but never talked to. That's my definition.''

"So maybe some guys you knew in school have it easy. What do you think it means to them? Nothing worth having or knowing comes easy. When it comes to you it might be worth something because it took its own sad time.''

"You think so?''

The eyes go dead again. "What do I know? Anyway, if you're desperate I know a couple of women would be glad to take part of your inheritance off your hands.''

"Who says I'm desperate?''

"These are women with whom I have occasional acquaintance, but you don't need my help. Right around where you live it shouldn't be too hard to find what you're after.''

"I never said I was after some whore.'' He laughs. "The old man calls them 'hoors'.''

"Let's say you get up the nerve one night, in a coffee shop uptown. *Pickup on Wilson Avenue*. Good title. You know Sam Fuller?''

"Is he a pimp?''

This time Sheffield laughs. "A director, something like Nicholas Ray only genuinely crazy. Start watching out for some of these guys, Dwight. Sam Fuller would do great things with you in some greasy spoon on Wilson, the night you went up to this lady, maybe she looked like Jean Peters but even wiser. She had to keep from laughing at the polite way you asked if she was available. Good thing she had a car, God knows you didn't. Her flat up in Rogers Park was cleaner than you expected, you felt safe there at least at first. On the el home though you realized you had never felt as alone as you did with her. You wondered how you could feel lonely when you were inside someone. The next night you went back, and the next. You started budgeting your inheritance, you wanted it to last so you could keep coming back. Things began to change. Each time you felt a little less lonely.

"After a while you tried to get her to tell you about her life. Your babble made her nervous, but you kept on telling her your life and asking hers. One day her pimp gave you a call, the voice of Lee Marvin warning you to lay off with all your questions. He must have figured you for a cop of some sort. Then you got mad: you were paying good money, you could talk all you wanted. So you started buying her presents, a clock radio, nylons, filet mignon. These only made your money run out quicker, and they didn't break her down.

"One night you told her all the different versions of her past you had dreamed up. If she wouldn't give you her story you'd give her several to choose from. All of them involved betrayal, so one of them had to be true. And then you asked her to come and live with you. She'd never have to work again, you'd find a good-paying job and keep her comfortable. You asked her straight out, lying there in the dark. She turned on the light. What would I do all day or all night? she asked you. How would I pass the time?

"And you put on your clothes and walked your few miles home."

Sheffield brings his coffee to his mouth one spoonful at a time.

"Where do you get all these stories of what could happen to me?"

"God knows," the man says. "But I have spent a lot of time at the Drake."

"Those things never happen in movies. You never see a man and woman lying in bed, at least not in the movies they show at the Drake."

"True enough. But I sure saw a lot of movies right across the street. Years ago. Today I wanted to come and see if the place had changed."

"Then why didn't you?"

The hatrack is almost bare.

"I told you. I took a fall. Went to bed at three last night, same as usual, woke up at eight, lay there thinking today I'd come to these movies with you, and when I sat up there he stood, grinning at me. First time I'd ever seen his face, and I was on my back, defenseless. His face didn't surprise me, I had figured all along it would be close to mine. But the grin was wrong, I never smiled in that frozen way. We shook hands. I got up, I shaved, but this time I felt such relief. Certainty. For the first time in seven years I knew I was going somewhere I wanted to go. The liquor store's only a block and a half from my room, right on Wells. All these years I'd forgotten how clean they keep that place. And the smell of a well-kept liquor store! Must be all that new glass, new labels. Clean cartons. A smell full of possibility."

"And now you're happy?"

"Relieved. Let it go at that. But sorry I messed up our get-together."

"You can go there anytime," Dwight says.

"Better with a veteran, someone who can show me the ropes."

"What ropes? The Drake is a movie theater. You buy your ticket and find your seat. To tell you the truth, I couldn't care less you didn't show up."

When Sheffield says, "You know that isn't true," Dwight looks up, ready to say Yes it is, I really don't care.

But then Sheffield says, "You wouldn't go to the Drake if it were the same as other places. You're like Edward G. Robinson, I mean Emmanuel Goldenberg, when he hides out in the monastery in *Brother Orchid*, and he can't believe how kind the monks are, and all he can say is, This dump ain't like other dumps! Well, that's the Drake. I started going there in the days right after I dried out. Dried out for good, I almost said. After I finished the painting, or didn't finish it, after my little nine-day ordeal. I had to find another job, but this took some time. I wanted something halfway decent. I knew I couldn't get an actual good job, what with how I had left Hacker and Wills and how I had spent the next four years. But still I was set on something better than cleaning toilets. So I made the rounds of the employment services. Each morning I'd go through the routine. A checkered professional history, was the euphemism I heard the most. Checkered liver, they should have said. Knowing me, you can imagine that one of these little encounters per day was quite sufficient. By noon I'd find myself in the Drake. Four straight months, five days a week, plus sometimes I snuck down on Saturdays or Sundays or both, got there earlier on weekends and saw each movie an extra time."

"You stayed all day?"

"Not always. Sometimes just until dark, some nights all the way. It kept me going. Every day I spent there made me one day dryer, one day stronger. Four months, two hundred movies, after three showings I could barely move, much less think about lifting a bottle. But the place kept drawing me back. I liked the blankness of the walls, and the people, most of them worse off than me, old or half-crazy or both. Drunks who could talk back to the screen for twenty minutes without repeating themselves. The Drake was even more of a home to them than to me.

"But after a while the movies began to wear me out. It wasn't only boredom, I started losing track of the weeks, I began to miss the actors when I went home at night. I couldn't remember the last time I had talked to anyone about anything other than my need for a job. The place became the job in itself but one I performed for free. And of course I was running out of money. The employment services could do zero for me. I was scared now, scared even of the Drake Theater.

"One morning I got into my weekday go-to-interview suit but when I stepped outside I started walking northeast, away from the Loop. Middle of May this was, but cold, a cold morning in May, nineteen fifty-six. Who knows what I had in mind, heading for the lake on a day that chilly? I never got there. On North Michigan I ran into my old boss from Hacker and Wills. We walked along a block or two. He tried not to act embarrassed. I remember I was wearing a hat because at a certain point I asked him to write me a reference and I took the hat off and I stood there with my hat in my hands, literally. I wanted him to pretend I had never walked out of that meeting. He couldn't hide his embarrassment anymore. To this day I believe he said yes just so I would put my hat back on. Which I did. And with that reference I got a job. Designing the auto parts and hardware sections of the Sears-Roebuck catalog, down on the Southwest Side. A decent job."

His cup clinks against the saucer. Dwight shifts on the sticky seat, not knowing, as they both wait here in the near silence of the coffee shop, what question he should ask this man sitting across the table hunched over his empty cup and half-full ashtray. The right question to ask next. The main one, the main question.

Dwight gets up. The man says, "He had such a cold handshake."

"Who? Your old boss?" Is this the main question, the main point?

"He wasn't really like me. My own hand almost froze to his. Here."

Sheffield holds out his hand. Dwight stands there. When at

last he takes the other's hand he can't believe how warm it feels. For just these few seconds, until their hands part, he can imagine the warmth of the other passing into his own self.

The morgue man takes the order slip from Dwight's hand. "Declaration of Independence, huh? What's your boss want to do, run the thing on page one of the Red Streak?"

"He's not my boss, and could you step on it?"

The man disappears. Waiting at the counter Dwight hears him moving back through the *D* section, muttering, "Donnybrook, Diphtheria, Dewey-Thomas, Dewey-John," then hears him say, "What do you mean, anyway?"

"The Declaration of Independence. July Fourth, you know? It starts in two hours."

"No, no, no, no. What do you mean, Victor Shields is not your boss?"

Though alone at the counter, Dwight shrugs. "My boss is Arthur Sheffield. Shields is temporary."

The man reappears with the file, shaking his head and smirking. "Sheffield is not coming back. They been looking for months to can that pissant."

"Missing two nights is no reason to fire him."

"Three nights."

"Monday night he called in sick," Dwight says. "So tonight makes the second night with no word."

This time the morgue man shrugs. "I'm not on the jury. For all I care they can give the pissant the Pulitzer Prize. I just know he's gone. Look at it this way: they're working their way through the alphabet. Up until two-odd years ago, a bimbo named Ike Sharpless was night editor. Then Arthur Sheffield. Now Shields. When they get to Zizzy Zyzzyzitsky we can all go free."

"Listen, Sheffield has done his best. He's stuck with lousy reporters."

"You noticed. But I thought your boss was in a hurry for this."

"Oh. Right, I better . . ."

His tie pulled down, the yellow collar of his shirt open, both arms in motion to snap his fingers for Dwight and slam down the phone, Victor Shields gives off an odor of stale coffee. "A file does not take ten minutes to go and get, kid, I don't care what you and that numbskull in the morgue were gabbing about."

Dwight knows that no matter what he says at this moment, he will sound impudent.

"Yes, sir." His voice is the voice of a wise guy. Shields waves a doughy hand in his face. "Don't start out smart with me. Go see what O'Donnell wants."

At ten thirty-five the boy stands at the east windows, considering the angles. What can he tell Shields that the man would believe? His best friend just got beaten up by the Blackstone Rangers, who happened to stray several miles north of their turf tonight? No, Shields would stick it on the front page: RACE WAR LOOMS! No. Dwight knows better than to try and pull off a lie. If the truth was good enough for Sheffield, it will have to be good enough for his substitute.

He strides to the desk of Victor Shields. "Mister—Sir? I'd like—I have to leave a little early tonight."

"What for?"

When Shields looks right at him he can feel the truth go under. In his moment of hesitation he wants to dive in and save it, but already he can hear unplanned words coming from his mouth.

"My grandfather's worse than usual tonight, when I called him he—"

"You called out on one of these phones?"

"Well, I had to, sort of, see, he's been sick a long time, and he was real bad when I left for work."

"Next time use a pay phone in the cafeteria."

Shields takes a sip of coffee from the cup he keeps under a box of paper clips. "Cold as a witch's . . ."

Dwight coughs. Without looking up Shields says, "Got a cold? Summer colds are the worst. You're all bone, kid. A man goes nowhere without some meat on him."

Dwight shakes his head, nods, shakes his head.

"You ought to lift weights or something."

"Uh-huh. So it's okay if I leave early?"

"Oh, I guess this once. If your old man feels that lousy he should check into Cook County General."

"He's not my father, Mister Shields. He's my grandfather."

"I stand corrected." Shields pulls a dollar from his shirt pocket. "Large. Get it back here before it turns to ice coffee."

Dwight puts the bill in his own shirt pocket. He doesn't want his own one thousand and seventy-three dollars to be disturbed. Before it turns to ice coffee! He walks a little slower. He watches his hand move to the knob on the door leading down to the cafeteria. His lips are moving, he wishes he knew what words they formed.

"Are you out of your mind?"

"Why?"

Already breathless, he stares back at the man in dark glasses who grants admission to the Drake. The marquee lights play against those glasses, against the ticket booth window and the man's gleaming head. In a patient voice the man explains: "Don't show off a wad like that in the Loop in the middle of the night. You never know who might be watching."

Turning to see if anyone is (no!) Dwight drops his handfull of bills. "Sorry," he says to no one in particular as he crouches on the warm, filthy sidewalk gathering his inheritance one more time. The night being almost windless, the bills wait to be taken up into his hands.

"My boss made me late." He stands again. "Shields, I mean. Except he isn't my boss." Very carefully he slides a ten into the man's hands. "He said he'd let me go early but then he kept me till two minutes of. So I wasn't thinking, I just wanted in to the movie in a hurry."

The man counts out his change. "Ticket machine's busted. No usher to take your ticket anyway."

When he steps over a man asleep in an aisle seat the man comes awake, shouting, "Lila!" From a few rows back comes another voice: "Sit down and shut up before I wring your turkey neck."

Making himself as small as possible, Dwight staggers to a seat at the end of the row.

Jimmy Cagney is sitting on his mother's lap. How did this come to pass? Silently the boy curses Victor Shields for making him miss the first fifteen minutes, the intricate series of steps leading to this mysterious scene. The sweat cold on his neck, he tries to make sense of the pictures before his eyes.

Back in that haven for hoors. I couldn't care one damn. What I can't stomach is him taking the money everyplace. Hasn't he learned a solitary fact in his seventeen years and six, seven, eight days? If I'd had the strength to watch him graduate, when they called his name I'd have stood up and said You can't let this one out into the world, you haven't cured him yet of his dumbness.

I will. Teach him the world. Tell him the little I've got to tell of Vera's life. Would that do it? Fix the blindness he stumbles around in?

Try.

Whatever wind wasn't dead at midnight is dead now. Down the alley stretching from behind the Drake to behind the junk shop and the steps leading down to the subway Dwight walks. The pulse in his temples, the echo of his footsteps, the images of Cagney all make him imagine he is walking very fast but whenever he looks up he seems not to be getting any closer to the alley's end.

Cagney, caught in the first knowing of his mother's death, jumps howling onto the mess table punching every guard who tries to haul him down. When he leaps from table to table he is trapped in that knowing. Dwight walks, walks. When Hazard dies will he react the same way? He'll be better off then and so will Hazard. The old man, free for good, and himself free to take his money and go. Not caught, not howling at anybody's dying, gone. A different Dwight Cope, this one left behind to walk this alley hearing a siren while the new Dwight Cope is free. This one left behind to listen to the tales of a reformed lush, now a formerly reformed lush who doesn't show up for work anymore. Once a lush always.

The sound of whose footsteps keep cutting into the dead night? If he isn't making any progress, who is? Or do these steps still echo his own? To walk faster like Cagney always. To not get caught. But even Cagney was. Caught even Cagney

∆ ∆ ∆

March the 23rd

Dear Vera,

Winters finely done, or these bags of wind won't last till Opening Day. A dry climates what I need, says Doctor Mejian. As if I never heard such advice. But hes not a bad egg for a doc even if he is some sort of a Turk. Patrice gave me the tip, he had done some good for her arthrytis. She asks after you too, so does Tommy. Did I tell you Alf went real sudden there last September? He wanted so bad to pass along the business to Tommy. But whoever heard of a blind plumber? and George won't be old enough to take over for another ten years. Alf never got over Tommy. He must of just given up. But Patrice kept her sense of humor. She brings me leftovers now and again. They still live close on Malden so its' no trouble she says. I dont like to except handouts, you might remember. From her I dont mind.

Cossum had the nerve to actually tell me would I go back on nights. I just looked at him. Even if we are getting ourselves hooked in another war. Please, he says. Please, Hazard. First time he ever said Please to me. Its' not like you have a family or anything. This had to make me laugh. Back when I had a daughter who needed me to watch over her you people couldnt care less I said, or I wanted to say. Finely I just said Look I like my life fine now. Which may not be the whole truth but Im too old to change my routine again. Days are work and nights are rest.

Tell your husband take it easy with the bottle. The both of you. Youve got somebody else counting on you now. Tell your husband from me.

Hi to the kid by the way.

PS. I got out the telegram you sent which for some reason I had saved it at the bottom of my sox drawer. Dwight was born 1:30 AM.

June 7th

Dear Papa,

I was glad to read your letter and that you're going to a doc after all this time. Pay attention to that advice about a dry climate. We've got an alright doctor for Dwight, though his health has been fine except those mumps last summer, but he does have a heart murmur which apparently came down from his daddy and anyway it never hurts to have a pediatrician handy. Raymond says Dwight's lucky, a heart murmur will keep him out of the service. His words came as a surprise, after all Ray's own dad went to the trouble of bribing some army doctor so Ray could enlist, which Ray used to say was one of the secret benefits of having a career officer for a father.

But once in a while he says things I wouldn't expect, such as we ought to raise Dwight in the church. He's getting to the age where he might grasp a little of what God means and we might as well start letting him know now about such things, and since Ray was raised something particular the Catholic church will do as well as any especially with so many around this area. This summer we'll start taking him to mass, or maybe just Raymond will, I'd feel odd not believing any of it. If Ray wants to make like he still does that's his business.

Last week at Sissy's (sometimes she comes out and takes him to their place for part of a day to give me a little break) he comes in from playing and says Aunt Sissy look what I found. And he opens his hands: a tarantula! Now the things are not as fatal as people make out but still I don't go for the notion of him making playmates out of them, if he did get bit he'd have a bad fever and hurt like the devil for days. If I'd been there I'd have screamed at Dwight holding on to it as if it was the most natural thing. Sissy did scream, Dwight dropped the spider, and he and Sissy and Angela spent the next two hours pushing him out from under the couch with one end of a broom and sweeping him out the door with the other. That night when I asked him how come he had brought the thing indoors he said To watch over him. As if a tarantula needs watching over by a going-on-four-years-old little boy.

The telegram should have said 1:30 p.m. I know, I was there.

The air's so dry and the days so clear sometimes I imagine the sky will never change but stay blue as a sheet of ice for good. Tell Doctor Mejian he's absolutely right.

Love, Vera

8.   The Wrong Picture

Dwight can see the old men walk toward him through the evening light. Six old men, or seven, his head hurts too much to count. These old men come out for the late editions of the *Patriot* or *Clarion*, with the Wall Street report and results of the first five races at Arlington. These men must be concerned with the races, not the stock market. But who's to say? The boy himself was hoarding a fortune until two o'clock this morning.

One by one they reach the newsstand and step forward. Passing the stand he looks away, to avoid the flash of coins, the bright covers of fifty magazines. He came out to get away from his grandfather's endless silence and to ease the dull roar in his head, not to see anything as bright as coins. He moves on so slowly that the old men from the Griffith Arms apartment hotel overtake him, eight old men saving the news for their evenings in the lobby, the coffee shop, the room. A year ago tonight he probably walked these streets and took no more notice of the old men than he did of any other routine sight. But since then he went to work at the *Patriot*, trading his own evening world for the world of the newspaper. Now he is following eight ghosts with newspapers back to their world.

7:18 by the Lucky Tiger clock in Lepcio's Barbershop. Dwight has killed barely an hour, but he can't go home yet to the unspoken rage of Hazard Harker. If only the old man had kicked him out, or pulled a razor and cut him bad enough to let out some of his own rage. If only he'd sworn at him for ten or twenty minutes. But when the boy came in this morning and told him what had happened, Hazard lay there clutching his blanket and staring into space and didn't even bother to look surprised. One of his hands made a tiny motion of dismissal. The voice came, cracked. "Put ice on your head. Get out of my sight."

All day he waited for sleep. The pain began to loosen its grip, the dizziness came back only when he got up for fresh ice. But his grandfather's silence demanded he stay awake. Was this what it was like to have something worth crying over? But his mouth, eyes, whole inside, whole self felt dry. The Cubs were home today for a Fourth of July doubleheader, and when no sound of the game came from Hazard's room at one o'clock, the silence pressed Dwight down on his bed.

Now he enters the Griffith Arms coffee shop, where five of the old men sit reading at five separate booths. "Large coffee to go," Dwight says. The waitress—no perfect white skin here either, no jet black hair—doesn't make a face at having to change his dollar but after taking the coins from the register she slams the drawer so hard his head starts to throb again. But as he drinks the coffee the muscles in his neck and shoulders begin to relax, as if released from the battle they've waged all day against one another, against themselves.

"Tomorrow I turn seventy-seven," says one of the old men to the waitress.

"Kudos to you, Sidney," she answers. "Come in for a free Blue Plate Special."

"I'll tell you one thing, though." Sidney puts his paper aside and speaks as if telling her the most important thing she will ever hear. "When you turn seventy-seven you really find out what's what. I've known it all along, been waiting for years. Tomorrow evening when I walk in here, Blue Plate Special or no Blue Plate Special, I'm going to know what existence is all about. It's coming to me on my seventy-seventh."

The waitress stands with the coffee pot held in front of her as though for protection against the seventy-six-year-old man's words. "You going to share your newfound wisdom with the rest of us, Sidney?"

"I don't know yet. That will come to me tomorrow too."

Ablaze with a happiness he has no right to feel, Dwight walks out to the busted fire hydrant in front of the coffee shop and taking easy sips of the lifegranting coffee he watches a line of hydrant-water slide along the curb. Tomorrow night he'll come back here to learn the newly seventy-seven-year-old man's truth. For something that important, he will have to miss work again. And tonight he will return to the Drake: not in hopes of catching the man who blackjacked him, a man he would have no way of recognizing; he'll go because he has looked forward to *Hail the Conquering Hero*, and now that he isn't working he can also see *Christmas in July*, both by Preston Sturges, another director Sheffield has told him to watch out for.

He starts walking to the Wilson el station. Is this why the old men live at the Griffith Arms, to be close to this coffee that makes you believe you're starting all over?

How many hours did she put in all told? Saved it over the years I made her work. What would she have done if those hours had been her own? Now they belong to some thief. Her hours. Get the boy back here. Shout down the windows till he hears you from blocks away. Tell him all you know. The hours she put in for those bonds. Grab his throat till he hears.

Let him go. If Jesus Christ couldn't save me from dying how can I save the boy from living the fool's life he's determined to lead or destined for? In some alley he went and lost her hours. No teaching him now.

The el is trundling towards Fullerton, last stop above ground, when Dwight notices the paper left on the seat behind him. He holds it up to what remains of daylight: Green Streak, the early afternoon edition of today's *Patriot*. Tonight he isn't working for a paper, tonight he could be anyone. Almost curious, he studies yesterday's box scores, examines the weather chart as if he himself didn't type it. How many hours ago? In the hours of his wealth. Now he turns back to the front section for what he doesn't already know, the stories that came in after midnight, chronicled while he was watching *White Heat* and walking down the alley and lying unconscious for what seemed, when he woke in the alley, to have been a full day and another night but had been only the few hours before dawn.

The picture of Sheffield appears in the bottom right corner of the front page. A stock picture in a newspaper, it holds no life. The face is so free of wrinkles, of character, Dwight has to look three times at the caption to make sure he knows this man. Knew him. Out of him comes a sound, half groan and half sob, that makes the woman in front of him turn around. Another sound would follow, Dwight chokes it down. The woman turns away. Dwight breathes again. One sound for Sheffield hangs in the air.

The caption, the picture, are wrong, cold, as cold as the shade's handshake. Stock photograph from the morgue man's file, an empty face. Here is the comfort: this picture is not the man. The lie is easier to take when they run the wrong picture alongside.

He doesn't turn to the obit. He knows the phrases. Why don't they print what Sheffield said? "NEWSPAPERS PRINT NOTHING," EDITOR QUIPS BEFORE SUICIDE. Why not make that the motto of the *Patriot*; not "Chicago's Freethinking Newspaper," but "Newspapers Print Nothing." Then people won't be disappointed to get nothing in return for their seven cents. Nothing, such as what the morgue man will say the next time Dwight goes down for a file: "Saw where your boss kicked the bucket on purpose." Such as the nothing Shields will say when he gives Dwight an order, Shields, who didn't tell Dwight the news when he called in sick this afternoon. Tomorrow night Dwight will be back there, obeying nothing. Before it turns to ice coffee.

Far underground now, stairways and escalators, next stop Madison/Monroe, the Drake; he blinks hard, trying to find living faces among the others in this car, peering for signs of life. The ones asleep look like trees or animals but at least alive, the ones awake like hunks of clay or bunches of old cloth. He doesn't get off the train. Closing his eyes he lets his paper slide into his lap where it becomes a blanket for his shivering legs, and he wishes for another cup of Griffith Arms coffee and wishes most he could draw another sound from his lungs.

Everybody gets left behind. The Girl in White knows, so she leaves the boy from Chicago behind in the small town. She knows because Sheffield told the story. He knew the story of Laura, left behind, he knew all the stories. Everybody says No. Like the whore said No to the boy or said No to Sheffield himself. Either way, whether he lived the story or not, he knew the ending. All the stories are about betrayal, so one must be true. The tale of Dwight's mother. The tale of Dwight, abandoned by the late Sheffield, a former ex-lush and teller of the same story over and over.

But Dwight's mother was not left behind forever. That was a mistaken notion caused by the Arizona sun and the loneliness of the night wind in the desert. Raymond Cope came back to stay. He had driven the stolen '49 Packard into Phoenix to sign up to fight in Korea. With his war record they made him a sergeant on the spot, shipped him hot into the heat of battle. He came out changed, a man at last, and home to his waiting wife and son he rode. Straight from the Centinela depot he takes them for a root-beer float and then to the movies: two grownup tickets, one child's. His son has grown no older in Sergeant Cope's absence, his wife no less lovely. Dwight's mother teaches him the stories in the hieroglyphics on the theater walls: the entombment of the Pharoah, his wife, his servants. His son must live on to take his place. Between movies the sergeant goes out for popcorn, wife and son sit waiting, the boy reading and reading again the symbols while he waits for his father to bring back refreshment. When the walls fly up and out the boy is amazed to find that night has fallen into the city, to find his mother and himself alone together under the night wind.

This time the el emerges into an area of scattered lights, warehouses, vacant lots, and new apartment buildings huger than any on the North Side. A few blocks away Comiskey Park can be seen, its tall banks of lights cold. Before he closed his eyes he was studying faces. Now the faces look back at him, the only white person in the car, puzzled faces, or hostile, or bemused. Stick close to home. Once, just after his grandfather brought him to Chicago, they went to Comiskey Park. Dwight shakes his head in the surprised remembering that his introduction to baseball came at Comiskey Park, not Wrigley Field. Why did they go to see the White Sox first? Weren't the Cubs the old man's team all along? Watching the dark stadium float past, Dwight can recall nothing of the game itself but high gray stands and more people than he had known could gather in one place.

Stick close to home: the words confused him all afternoon. The man kept trying to explain the rules of baseball, kept pointing to a spot called "home," and if it was way over there on the other side of the field, too far away even to be seen, how could Dwight stick close to it? Yet every time he ran down for a closer look at the relievers warming up in the bullpen, his grandfather called out the same thing. The words play through his head now from all the times the old man has said them, whenever Dwight started a new year at school or the first time he rode downtown alone to the Field Museum. And when they went together to see the Dodgers or the Giants play the Cubs, Hazard would point out that "a lot more coloreds" came out to see those two teams, so Dwight should stick close to home.

What was the old man afraid "all these coloreds" would do if Dwight lingered too long in their midst? Meanwhile Hazard went on rooting for the players who brought out these fans, Ernie Banks, Willie McCovey, Maury Wills, Roy Campanella before his car crash, Jackie Robinson—"the first colored ever"—and Willie Mays—"the greatest ever, colored or otherwise." Would he be terrified now at Dwight's riding through the South Side night, past Comiskey Park where they sat in the centerfield bleachers once twelve years ago surrounded by all these colored? At Grimm he heard them referred to by many names. And nowadays most people on the *Patriot* say "Negroes," lately the boy has heard talk of hiring a "Negro" reporter. So how should he think of them? Maybe one word isn't enough. Maybe he should think of them as, "The people who were never close to what the old man called home." The people who are never close to home.

The *Patriot* lies at his feet, the not-picture of Sheffield crumpled. Dwight will ride to the end of the line, where the el turns around; he has never ridden that far. Back through the same territory he'll come, secretly watching the faces change or looking out at the fireworks beginning now over the lake. He will press his face to the glass, barely able to catch the rockets in their soaring and their bursting, fading.

The morgue man winks at someone behind Dwight. The boy turns from the counter to find O'Donnell staring back at him from the doorway. The morgue man says, "Kid here wants a file on his late great boss."

O'Donnell's eyes grow even narrower. "What are you up to, son? You're supposed to be sick."

"My name's Dwight."

"If I'd known you were here I wouldn't have had to come down."

The morgue man gives his strangled shout. "Do you believe this guy, O'Donnell? He wants us to call him Mister Cope!"

"I never said that, you stupid creep."

Startled by his own words, mystified by his own presence here on this strange and apparently endless night when he should be home sleeping off the loss of his inheritance, his future, Dwight goes on: "All I said is I don't want to be called son anymore. Or kid, or boy. You guys aren't my father. You don't give a damn what happens to me."

"I care plenty," the morgue man says. "What I'd most like to happen is for you to imitate your pal Sheffield and go croak yourself with a bottle of Irish."

"He drank himself to death?"

The morgue man laughing is an event Dwight has never witnessed. When at last he comes up for air he says, "I got to hand it to you, kid, you do at least have an imagination. Nobody dies from one fifth of Irish, not even a nobody with Sheffield's liver. The stuff's only eighty proof. I'm talking about what doesn't get printed in the paper. I'm talking about he broke the bottle and sliced away at his throat till he didn't have anything left to slice away at."

Dwight stares at him until the gleam in the morgue man's eyes makes him turn to the other man for denial. O'Donnell shakes his head. "Some things you should keep to yourself."

"What do you care, O'Donnell," the morgue man says, "you never had a good word for the guy."

"I know I didn't. But the kid. You shouldn't have told him."

"I'm not a kid," Dwight says quietly.

He wishes only that no one will walk in on him, not because of the mild foolish embarrassment he feels when someone enters while he is standing at the urinal but because the pain of crying surprises and shames him: the dumb flow of tears and mucus, the shaking in his chest, these things physically hurt, especially when he is trying at the same time to rid himself of the Griffith Arms coffee shop coffee.

He gets his wish: nobody interrupts him. The boy is free, as he stands at the sink splashing water into his face while the tears just keep on coming down, to wonder why he wasn't there to talk Sheffield out of it. Why isn't Sheffield here now to say, You were right not to believe the picture: That wasn't me: I'm not part of the nothing newspapers print.

Dwight crosses the city room and taps his boss lightly on the shoulder.

"Mister Shields?"

He can feel the same scared politeness begin to pull him down as it did when he spoke to Shields last night. The man looks up at him as if to get this over with.

"It's hard," Dwight says. "I kept riding the el back and forth. I'd get off at one end, go down and pay my way back up to the outbound platform. I had all this change. Isn't that funny? Lost a cool thousand but still had a pocket full of quarters. Sheffield would have thought that was funny. Did you know Sheffield? He thought a lot of things were funny."

"Do you have a fever on top of your cold, son? That what's troubling you?"

"Anyway, I had enough change to go on riding all night, but the third time that southbound pulled into Grand I jumped out, I wanted to come and see about Sheffield, find out what doesn't get printed in the paper like the morgue man says. But did you know Sheffield? It's hard to believe any of you did. Not that I did either. Come to think of it I don't even know what I'm talking about. Maybe I should just shut up. Maybe everybody should. You know what I mean, Mister Shields?"

His boss returns to marking a piece of copy. "You need a rest, boy. Why don't you get started on it right now?"

"Mister Shields? I was gone a long time ago."

Walking back across the city room he tries to remember from what movie his last words came. They came from no movie, or at least none he has seen. They are his own, the right words for this particular exit.

The lights of the *Patriot* building bob and swoop along the black waves of the river. Crossing the bridge he can see by the giant clock above the County Jail that he will easily make the last showing of *Hail the Conquering Hero*. He can walk slowly along the streets that have not changed since last night, free of his first full-time job. How will they live? On the old man's Social Security and the one hundred dollars Joan Fontaine persuaded him to leave in savings?

When he goes to take out that hundred he will stand in line again at her window.

Nearer to the Drake he starts to run, past dark windows of living-room furniture, chocolates in pale blue boxes, pawned cameras, the junk shop where nothing of equal value has replaced the blinking heart of Jesus. Is he running to make the opening credits or so as not to know what a thief does if his victim turns out to be carrying only a few grimy coins? By the time he approaches the ticket window he is running so hard, and fishing out his sixty cents so clumsily, that he barely notices the sign in the window. Bending over to gather his breath, he is hit by the words: USHER WANTED.

△ △ △

October the 21st

You can partly thank Patrice for this. The money comes from yours truly. But shes the one pointed out your 5th anniversary must be coming. Sending you a present for this feels funny. At 1st I wasn't sure if you had done the right thing. But 5 years must mean something. Just be sure and use it wisely. You could save out part for a Christmas present later on for Dwight. That's up to you.

Hazard (Pa)

Came across that old music box, you remember? Still doesnt work right. Youll get it in a seprate package.

November 2

Dear Papa,

I wouldn't have thought Patrice knew our anniversary. Your present came as a real surprise, anyway, one happy surprise. I hope you'll thank her for me as well as taking our thanks yourself. I had never even seen a hundred dollar bill before, not that the amount matters. I hope I don't have to say anymore for you to know how I feel.

Love, Vera

November 7

Pa,

After your present I feel awful asking this but we're in a little fix as far as the house is concerned, we've fallen one payment behind and if you could see your way clear to a loan of another 100 it would make all the difference. This is a once only request. If I thought we could turn to someone else but Leo already gave Ray a couple advances on his salary in the past and couldn't do more without Marv catching on. I've gotten a job at Sammy's, a diner in Centinela. My only worry is leaving Dwight off with Sissy, I don't want him to be a burden on her.

Almost time for work so I'll end here with thanks in advance
if you can help out. It just seemed to creep up on us.

Love, Vera

P.S. The music box arrived though sorry to tell it must have
been damaged further in transit and now plays only about
two-thirds of the tune instead of almost the whole thing. Maybe
when we're back on our feet we can fix it. Meantime I can hum
or whistle the rest. Thanks for sending it, I must have forgotten
it back when.

November the 16th (Tuesday)

I'm sending this Air Mail. But you can forget calling it a loan.
I'm enough taken care of to afford a few bucks. It was tough to
figure how you could get yourselfs in a hole if he's the great
popular mechanic. But then what with the price of food today
and raising a kid and all. Put paying me back out of your mind.
Try and be a little more careful is all.

Pa

Day before Thanksgiving

The money arrived safe and sound and now so are we.
Thanks, Papa. I'll write you a real letter soon, I promise.

Vera

Pa,

How do you like this card? One of the girls at the settlement
house run by the Church made it by hand. The Church sells
them to raise money for the house. Be sure you don't open the
present till Christmas morning (You're on your honor since I
can't be there)

Here's a snapshot of our house too. Well not of the house exactly but out back. This view was taken months ago but things look pretty much the same out there all times of year.

Love, Vera

(and Dwight and Raymond)

Vera,

I thought you could use this little extra. Call it half a be-lated gift from last Christmas and half this year's. Went out and bought a box of these cards. Hope you like the picture, youll be seeing it the next 11 years. The same farm house and all the same family coming home in the slay.

Your Pa

9. Depot

Hazard Harker searched for a sign. The train granted him time to panic: his nap had carried him past the right town, his grandson would know him first as a man who could not be relied on. He took a final draw. Returning the flask to his heart's pocket he heard the brakes cut high into the evening quiet and braced for the moment of full stop. He caught sight of a black-haired boy standing between a woman and a man beside the tracks. A few feet away a girl stood as if alone but staring at the woman. Over their heads a long wooden sign hung on rusted chains swung gently in the train's wake: CENTINELA.

Holding tight to his satchel he stepped very slowly down on the gravel. For a moment the coral air of dusk make him wonder if he might still be asleep. How could air take on this color? How could a place where people lived take on such quiet? For a moment he imagined the woman to be his own daughter, close set eyes, wheat colored hair. Then she stepped forward and took his hand. "Mister Harker." When he saw her eyes were blue he knew she was a stranger.

"Hazard. You can—"

"I'm Sissy Whalen. This here's my husband Leo and my daughter Angela."

The husband gave him a thin smile. Patches of sweat stood out on his yellow shirt. The wake of the train, seeming to depart in silence, lifted the woman's hair back from her neck, while the girl went on staring at her: the way a dog waits for a command,

Hazard thought. A red line of ants moved into the space between the girl's shoes.

He didn't want to look right at his grandson. After a night, a day, a night, and most of a day on the train he had not thought of a thing to say to the boy.

"Guess she was a little late," he said to Leo. "More than a little."

"I've seen her worse," Leo said. "Seen her five hours."

When Sissy shaded her eyes they grew larger, giving her face an expression of surprise. "Dwight wasn't too fretful, were you, Dwight?" She ruffled the boy's hair and spoke as if confiding in Hazard: "I told him a story to keep him occupied."

At last Hazard looked at his grandson. The boy clutched a cigar box: *Perfecto Garcia*, a better brand than Hazard himself smoked. Who did the boy know who smoked *Perfecto*? Now Dwight opened the box, holding it so that only he could look inside. Hazard wanted to take two steps and look over his shoulder to discover what treasures lay there. The boy looked up at him, and though he couldn't find words he made himself smile at this child who reminded him of nobody, not even of the boy in the pictures sent by his mother. *Perfecto Garcia*. A film of red dust lay across the box, and on the boy's light blue T-shirt, faded green shorts and white socks. But his brown shoes gave back flashes of the declining light. How in the world could they shine so in this place? He looked from the shoes to the sun, setting among the foothills beyond the tracks.

The wetness in his palms: rye whiskey or sweat? Both, it had to be both.

"So peaceful here," he heard himself say.

Turning his back to the shower head he stood shivering, enjoying the clear shock of the cold spray against his shoulders and spine and ribs. He reached behind him and turned the cold water higher and aimed the head against his lower back. It did nothing for the twists of pain but he liked the feel of something cold in this country.

Alice, ready with a tub to wash him back to life in early morning, her thin hand pulling the brush across his back. Thin Alice, big. Big with, great with their son.

Next came a girl but at least she lived. Whose son looked too much like his father.

Suddenly the water turned hot, Hazard moved to open the cold tap as wide as it would go while the water grew hotter still.

Brush. Thin hand. Alice great with Vera. Who at least lived.

The morning of the evening she ran away, she fixed ham and eggs and fried potatoes for herself, coffee so strong he smelled it all the way down in the gangway before starting up the back stairs. When he walked into the kitchen there she sat. Vera's last morning. Wednesday, had to be, Cubs beat Detroit in the opener, the Series always starts on a Wednesday. The cold light in her eyes while she ate that breakfast. He would see her again only in pictures. Or would see without seeing the odd half-smile she used to give him all of a sudden sitting in the front room on summer evenings listening to Tommy Dorsey. Her hands moving carefully to rearrange the treasures of her room, chunks of colored glass, rocks from the beach. Vera, who at least lived.

There. Done. Stepping back he turned and lifted his head to wash his own salt from his eyes. No one would know. They'd take the redness beneath his eyes for sunburn.

Done. The pain in his legs when he tried to take a deep breath reassured him. Salt washed down from his eyes with the sweat of his journey, he was himself again.

The Whalens' house sat in a dead end. In the darkness Leo watered what lawn they owned. Through the open front door Hazard could hear the slow fall of liquid. He stood in the kitchen doorway watching Sissy make supper, watching Dwight and Angela crouch near the big radio in the living room corner. Leo's gray form moved past the screen door, drawing the hose through the night in slow arcs. Dwight turned the dial slowly, as if listening for a particular station. Most of what came out was silence.

Angela pointed to the dial. "There."

Dwight shook his head. "That's nothing."

In Chicago you'll find a dozen stations, more, sound everywhere you turn. A radio I fixed myself, did your mother ever tell you?

He wondered if the boy had ever seen a television. Once maybe his mother had taken him into Phoenix where he had stared in wonderment outside the window of a department store, his dark eyes wide.

"—don't believe he quite understands." The woman was speaking to him. "We had to tell him something, Leo and I. Your mommy's gone away, we said. A couple of times he's cried for her. What can we say? He doesn't know what it means. How could he? A boy his age."

Dwight turned and looked up right at Hazard, and the man stepped back into the kitchen, out of the boy's sight. Some time, not tonight, later, perhaps on the train home, he would have to say "Never." Would the boy know what that meant?

Over supper, without realizing, he stared at Dwight until the boy looked up. Except for the tired turning of the floor fan, the room was quiet.

"Son," Hazard said, so suddenly that Angela looked up too. Her unfocused eyes scared him. "Son, we're going back to Chicago. Where the Cubs play."

His grandson's eyes pierced his own. The baseball team, the city, must mean nothing to him. The old man wondered why he had thought these words would matter. His voice empty of breath, he said, "It'll be your new home. Day after tomorrow we start back. Ever ride that train?"

"No."

Sissy was cutting Angela's steak. "Shame to leave so soon. I sort of figured you might want to stay a while, Hazard. After such a long trip."

The fan sent its lukewarm breeze against the napkin he had tucked into his collar. On the sideboard behind Sissy he saw for the first time a framed photograph of herself and Leo and Angela. In the picture Sissy looked so young she seemed to be posing in her wedding outfit as a joke. Angela had to be her kid sister, Sissy was too young to have a daughter of four or five. Now when he looked at her she no longer reminded him in any way of his own daughter. Now she seemed middle-aged, tired, a woman with a half-grown daughter and tired eyes.

"Real kind of you," he said. "But Dwight better see his new home soon. Besides, our tickets are for Friday."

"No trouble changing those. And if you stay a while we could show you some beautiful country. Couldn't we, honey?"

Leo finished chewing a piece of steak. "Well, now, Sissy, the plans seem all set."

In the silence Hazard watched Dwight push the lima beans around on his plate. He said, "I need to get back to work. There's that. They let me take the week with no notice. I can't stretch it."

"I can understand that," Leo said. "What sort of work do you do?"

"Machinist."

"Leo," Sissy said. "You know what Mister Harker does. Vera must have told us a hundred times."

"That's right," Leo said. "She did."

Sissy got up then and began to clear the table. Hazard said,

"A long time ago I worked in the mine." He spoke as if one giant mine lay beneath the whole world.

"I'll be darned," Leo said.

Angela said, "I'll be darned," and started clicking her tongue.

"What about you, Dwight? Would you like to rest a while more before you get on the train?"

Sissy stood in the kitchen doorway, the turning blade of the fan reflected in the long blade of the knife in her hand.

What the hell right does she have asking the boy what he wants?

You're a guest here. Keep your mouth shut.

"Stop that with your tongue, Ang'," Sissy said, and her daughter obeyed.

Again the woman asked, "What would you like to do?"

Dwight squashed a lima bean on his plate. "Go home."

Angela laughed once, loud. In the silence Sissy said, "Sshhhh."

Hazard knew the boy meant the home no one could give back to him. When he looked at Sissy he saw her gazing not at Dwight but back at him, and he thought Her eyes are blue as ice, and wondered where the thought came from.

The living room was lit by a cool sun. With a vaguely pleased surprise he realized he had gone to sleep immediately upon stretching out on this hide-a-bed last night and could not recall a single image from his sleep. Maybe he hadn't dreamed a thing. Maybe he had slept lucky.

A crow came and settled into the lone tree in front of the house and took up its call. Hazard nodded at the passing of that strange, gentle moment of waking.

When he woke again—or after one simple closing of the eyes, so that he couldn't tell if he had dreamed the lizard atop the radio or seen or pretended to see it in that moment of closing—Dwight stood at the window. As if with lives of their own, his hands kept opening and closing. Hazard sat up. A cough took him, then several, racking through him and out and through him again. The boy turned to him, turned back at the crow's take-off, stood watching the bird's flight across the yellow field, hands opening and closing again while his grandfather regained his breath.

"Glass of water?" Hazard said.

Dwight remained at the window until long after the man thought the crow must be out of sight. Then he ran to the kitchen, where he let the water run and run. He came back in very slowly, having filled the glass to the top. They both stared at the surface of the water as the boy came forward.

"I made it get cold."

When Hazard had taken a few sips he lay back down, closing his eyes once more. When he opened them for the third time he was alone.

This box held her. This pine box would travel on the same train, to Chicago and its proper burial. He had done every proper thing. Come to Centinela to claim his grandson, to this undertaker's to get this box to put on tomorrow's train. But what did it matter where she got buried?

In Chicago he could visit. That was proper, holding the boy's hand in front of the grave on a Sunday afternoon. Buy flowers cheap at the Hi!Neighbor. But a growing boy had better things to do than stand at his mother's grave. Hazard would bring her flowers on his own.

Last night, early this morning, he had dreamed, or heard, a freight train shunting along the tracks, metal on metal in the copper air of dawn. A sound wheels made bearing nails and flowers. Tomorrow this box would be freight.

The nails gleamed in the late morning light. A gentle cough:

the undertaker stood his respectful distance. Would Mister Harker care to step in and sign the necessary? Young, taller than Hazard, a handsome young undertaker, standing back in respect, in respect of what? Hazard slid his hand across the planed surface of the box and ran the few grains of sawdust through his hair.

The gray hood of the Centinela County Patrol car pushed through the night. How could Leo see to drive down this black highway?

Where do they keep the lights in this state?

Leo said, "She's a real beaut, isn't she?"

"Who?"

"This Plymouth."

"I don't know cars much."

"This car's the best thing about this job, which isn't saying much."

"You're not partial to it?"

Leo shrugged. "Had to find something after I lost the filling station. One time I thought Ray Cope and I would own the place. If I hadn't let myself get cheated, maybe things might have worked out different for all concerned." He flicked a fly away from his ear. "Maybe, maybe, maybe."

The fly struck the windshield again and again. Maybe if that son-in-law had had a place to call his own he wouldn't have run out. But what about his wife and son, why hadn't they been enough? No, if a man was a piece of scum you couldn't blame it on one missed opportunity. And if a girl made the dumb mistake of pinning her hopes on him she deserved what she got. Hazard didn't want to hear about it, anyway, didn't want to see the wrecked car or the accident report filled out and signed by Centinela County Patrolman Leo Whalen.

HOBART. POP 500. Out here even a slab of desert gets to be called a town. Minus her husband, four hundred ninety-nine minus Vera, four hundred ninety-eight, minus Dwight—

He didn't want to hear about it, and still he hoped to find some object in the house that would tell him how she had felt. When she watched her boy get on the school bus, had that parting seemed like any other or did she know this would be her last sight? Hazard stared at the purple shapes of mountains ahead where the road seemed to end, did not, went on twisting toward the place where her car had left it behind.

Out of control. Had to be. Life is not something a mother throws away one afternoon. A mother holds to life, a mother whose child looked to her for signs.

"Hogwash," he heard himself say, and then Leo said, "Beg pardon?"

"Oh. Was I talking out loud?"

That goddamn magazine, *American Way*, left behind by some other jerk who had ridden coach through the same empty towns, dead land. It had held part of his mind for a few hours on the train, now he found those lines on the glory of motherhood returning. In the end the child looks to its mother for the light of life. Were those the words? Mother, vessel of sacrifice.

Hogwash.

He looked at Leo to see if this time he had kept the word to himself. As the car climbed a rise in the road and came down he closed his eyes. The wheels made no noise. How could he trust a machine that twisted his insides without a sound? On the train his ears had let him know he was moving in the dark. In this car only the turning in his stomach told him he was riding through darkness to the place of their place, hers, the place of her and her husband, ex-, not-husband. The place that would tell him what he wanted to know and didn't.

Or won't tell me one thing.

Leo was pointing. Hazard turned, there, at the end of a dirt path, a gray box.

House of my daughter.

When Leo opened the front door Hazard felt heat swarm out of the house. He stepped back for a breath of wind before going in, pulse drumming through his temples while Leo stumbled around the room. At some point the light came on: yellow walls, blistered, the cheap brightness faded from the lumps and sticks of furniture. All she still owned, had owned. Had had. The bank would take back the house but the furniture was hers. His now. The Whalens would take the trouble of selling it, send him the proceeds. He shook his head, dizzy with bewilderment at the trouble people went to for other people.

The open door to the broom closet revealed an ironing board leaning against the wall, its torn cover hanging halfway to the floor. No sign here. In the kitchen, the bathroom, the child's bedroom: dust, spiders, the same yellow blisters. No hint, no sign, of his daughter. This place could belong to anyone.

He stood alone in her bedroom, theirs, full of the shuddering heat. The standup lamp gave what light it could. On the dresser he found, lying flat on its face, a framed picture of the three of them: one she had never sent him, taken in one of those studios, perhaps a year ago to judge by Dwight. How many days this past year had her so-called husband lived in this house, made himself available for a family portrait? The boy grinned right at the camera, framed by mother and father looking off in different directions, the father also smiling, the smile almost merging with the scar beneath his eye.

This was the face that had talked Vera into running away: on the handsome side, even with that scar, but no life in the eyes. Living with Hazard Harker had made the girl run off with this man, these eyes.

The wind made the paper rattle against the stone.

He looked more closely: on the woman's cheek, a mark, the kind of bruise she used to get when Hazard hit her. Or this might be a spot on the photograph. He couldn't tell, or didn't want to know. A mark: life with Hazard Harker.

One October morning he stretched out on his bed and went right to sleep, the same as usual after a night at the plant, and when he woke in the afternoon a humid breeze blew in against the note she had left on his bureau. The paper slapped the fat black stone holding it down, stone from her treasure of bright things found over the summers.

—The light seeping into this room—pigeon on my ledge—I'll always be your daughter—

In his boxer shorts and T-shirt he stood, reading. All right, she had run away from home, eloped to hell with a stranger, but where did the light fit in, or the pigeon? Hearing a fly just behind his ear he didn't swat it away. In her room in the night, he found, beneath the picture, a pink envelope. In his own room in daylight he read her note to him again. Holding the envelope up to the lamp he saw her son's name written in her hand, breaking open the envelope he asked himself if the fly had buzzed behind his ear a moment ago or six years ago. In one room his hands were steady, in another they shook. Into one room the breeze blew, into another came no trace of air. The pink paper rattled in his shaking hands. He moved it nearer the lamp. In his own room his hands remained steady even when he read again the words that told him she must be crazy. The idea of her craziness possessed him more strongly than knowing she had left him. Now the craziness in her words to her son made his hands shake.

—Call of the train whistle—hawk motionless in the bluest sky—when you outgrow this sweater give it away you won't need to save useless things to remember me by I'll be with you no matter—

Her words held him rigid by the lamp, and before the

window's breeze. No matter how many times he read these words he would not understand them. Wanting to forget them already he read them again. From a corner of her room or a corner of his the fly buzzed. He heard it while he read them over. With these words she made him alone, left him her words alone, then left him words to pass on to another who would make him no longer alone. He coughed, coughed again or twice more: in which room? The mother, true vessel of sacrifice, to whom the child turns, the girl who would write the crazy words turned to him as her child to her, as her child would turn to him now. Because in the course of events she had grown up without a mother, because now the boy would too and the boy now without a father, in the course of her mother's event, his mother's event. Leaving one man to pretend to be a guiding light, pretending for the girl until she ran off with a stranger who punched her face, took her, left her to take.

Read again. He had been no light. Till she left him with words. The stranger took her and left her to take her own. Face punched like a time clock. By the gray face he punched out, 6:02 AM. What time had she passed beyond the city limits? Where would she be by now on this Thursday afternoon? And on this Thursday night where now? He folded the letter. Crumpling her note into a damp ball in his fist he tossed the ball into the gangway. Folded the letter again, coughed, again. A truck could be heard down the alley. He heard himself cough. A man's voice called his name and he folded the letter. The truck faded away on a Thursday afternoon of no consequence except Game Two in Detroit, the Cubs sending Wyse against Trucks. The voice called again from another room. He coughed, or again.

Asking was he all right in here Hazard.

His lungs burned. Holding himself silent he slid the letter, folded three times, into his pocket. As he had found it he turned down the grin of the boy, the scarred face of the father, the mother's marked face. A picture of strangers in a strange house, lost now. A house without a sign of why she had. How he was to live. Be a light for her child.

Slowly the foothills rose, seeming to sail forward but never coming closer. Out there a car had been destroyed, and the body inside pried loose for shipment. He shivered. Boulders, limbs of cactus, grew from the black pool of ground. Slowly the pool itself came alive, gray scrub, the pale red sand. Sunlight, gray, not yet warming, struck his eyes.

Orphanage. For Dwight's sake. How could the man hope to light a path for the boy if the man had never been able to find a path himself? An orphanage could teach him to live among other people, live like other people, a place in Chicago where his grandfather could come see him, take the kid to the beach, to ballgames. Hazard would look around. A good place.

The sun came warmer. He shivered.

When he turned around, Sissy stood at the stove fixing a pot of coffee. "Thought you might like a thermos for the train."

He sat at the kitchen table. "Then I'll fix some lemonade, too," she said. "For Dwight."

"You've done so much for us already."

"We're really doing nothing. Vera was—well, this is nothing. Now what about clothes? He never needed real winter clothes down here."

"She made him a sweater. I found it last night." She stared at him. "I found it out there, at their house. A heavy sweater, for Chicago winter."

She sat at the table, saying nothing. In a few moments she got up. "I'll fix the lemonade."

But after slicing a lemon she stopped and came and sat again. The scent of lemon drifted through the kitchen. He tried to take a deep breath, and couldn't, the room had become so hot. In her bedroom Angela began humming a song that seemed to have no tune. Suddenly in this morning light he found he wanted to put his arms around the woman, have her put her arms around him, the two of them to lie down together on the kitchen floor. It might be cool down there. While her daughter's tuneless song went on he studied the curve of the woman's neck.

She said, "I wondered if it was true. An accident."

She could have said anything, any words and he would have wanted her all the more. His desire made him laugh.

She said, "There's never anything to say, is there?"

To make sure they didn't move, he placed his hands on the table, flat.

"Anyway," he said. "The boy will have a warm sweater."

Dwight crouched on the floor beside the armchair where Leo sat polishing his own shoes. As Leo finished with a brush or a cloth he handed it to Dwight, who repeated the action on his own shoes. Hazard stood watching the awkward movements of his grandson's hands.

"What do you say?" Leo said. "Kid learns fast, doesn't he?"

Hazard leaned down, pointing. "Missed a spot, Dwight."

"Where?"

"There, in the curve of the heel. No, the other shoe."

Dwight took up the other shoe and went to work.

The box was loaded into the baggage car by a heavy man with a face full of purple freckles while Hazard and Dwight and their hosts stood on the platform.

Does he know who it is? Does he know it's a who? I'll tell him. Have to.

Hazard heard a call that sounded more like "Oh no" than "All aboard!" Still he stood as though waiting for something dramatic to happen. There had to be something to say or do that would make their departure less awkward, after all this.

"Thanks for teaching him to shine his shoes," he said.

"Good thing to know," Leo said.

"I can shine mine, too," Angela said.

Sissy said nothing.

Even after they boarded the train the boy held tight to his cigar box and his silence. Hazard gave him the window, and watched the boy look out at the three people waiting in the morning shadows. Hazard envied them their shade. In a few minutes they'd go back to a house with a fan, where the air was breathable. On the trip down he had held himself to half the whiskey in his flask. Now he couldn't imagine drinking the half he had saved. For two days his only relief from the stranger beside him, and from the heat, would be sleep. If sleep came.

Dwight stood and pressed his forehead against the window and waved. Angela called out something the man could not understand. "Be careful"? The train had begun to move, then Hazard jerked forward when it all at once halted. It jerked forward, he fell back.

"Aunt Sissy isn't waving." Dwight said.

Hazard looked out. Angela hád turned her back and was buckling and unbuckling her shoes. Leo was moving his forearm up and down in a distant gesture, as if the train had gone and he was waving at air. Sissy did not look up. For all the man could tell she might have been counting pebbles in the weeds. He started to raise his hand, then let it fall. Why wouldn't she look up? He pushed his face to the heat of the glass to catch a last sight of the woman who stood there, head bowed.

"I think I forgot to say goodbye," Dwight said, and he started to cry. Hazard turned and said, "Sshhh," then sat motionless. The boy's crying grew no louder. He sat down awkwardly, as if tired of his own crying, and in a little while he did stop. Still he kept hold of his box. Still the old man didn't move.

The train began to gather speed as if the bare countryside were its only fuel.

Where's the kid?

The cigar box sat on the empty seat. Without hesitation Hazard opened it: an empty pack of Lucky Strikes, the heel of a grown man's shoe, two Indian Head pennies, a Secret Command glow ring, a tiny plastic dinosaur missing one leg, a rubber ball with almost all its coating peeled away, the partly decomposed corpse of a fly—which he picked out and dropped on the windowsill with other corpses—and two torn box-tops from Post Toasties. One item surprised him: a single earring, small, gold, leaf-shaped. How had the boy come to carry around one gold earring in this cigar box full of junk?

Kids don't know the value of a thing.

At the approach of the porter he slammed down the lid. The porter gave him a quick puzzled glance. Carefully he put the box back on Dwight's seat, then opened it once more to stare at the earring. It gave back the sun. From the sun's position he guessed he had slept at least an hour. Shutting the box again he started to reach for his flask, then let his hand fall and made himself get up and start down the aisle. On an almost empty train he should have no trouble finding him.

The smell of the diner, the low voices of the few people who had come to breakfast, made him dizzy. When he reached the door of the baggage car he knew the boy had to be back the other way, when he turned and started back his own movement against the train's made him stand with his head bent into his palms for a few moments. Then he forced himself on, back through the diner, the sleeper cars, past lines of empty coach seats, including their own. Entering the last car he could hardly feel his feet touch the floor.

Dwight stood on the rear platform. Stumbling forward Hazard stopped, started again.

Where in the goddam hell's the conductor leaving a five-year-old boy to stand back there where one sharp curve could shoot him off into the rocks?

He grabbed the handle and pulled so hard the door almost knocked him over. Then came the hot wind. The boy faced west, arms spread wide. Hazard wanted to hold him to his old jacket, old chest, wrap him inside his old smell. He wanted to whisper, Your mother knit you a sweater for Chicago.

Dwight stood with his mouth open. Watching him, silent as the boy was silent, Hazard wondered if he couldn't breathe. To the grandfather the boy seemed to be drinking the wind, letting the wind save his life.

January 11
Dear Papa,

You shouldn't have sent more money at Christmas, you've given us so much lately I start to feel bad. I shouldn't say that, I should just leave it at thanks. But pretty soon we plan to start paying it back, I hope for a raise soon at Sammy's. In fall Dwight starts kindergarden and Sissy won't have to take care of him while I'm working. Around where we live there still aren't many kids, I worry about him being lonely. What goes on in his head? Last Saturday morning the three of us were supposed to go for a drive but Ray wanted to sleep it off (Friday night with Leo) so it ended up Dwight and me driving up into the foothills where the road starts to get real steep and came to this little gorge with a creek running through. Usually it's dry but last week not, we had a storm before Christmas and another last week. We sat by the side of the road. Up and down that creek a half a dozen kinds of wildflowers grew. Up there I felt wide awake in the wind and the water sound. Dwight all of a sudden says "What do you call those flowers?"

"Which ones?"

"All of them."

Of course I didn't know, I never knew flowers. But if you come and visit I'll learn them all ahead of time so we can take you to that place.

I'm going to teach him to read. I don't really know how, you could say I should leave it to the teachers, but why wait if he's ready now?

Anyway Ray and I will start paying you back soon even if you didn't mean it to be a loan.

Love, Vera

P.S. Let me ask you something. Do you remember my mama being happy? Most of the time? Lately I wonder about her. Write and tell me something, if she used to laugh a lot or something.

Feb. the 16th

Dear Vera,

Here I've been enjoying the scarf all this time and its taken me 2 months to agnowlege it. But then winters get me down. Don't go taking this church business too serious with the kid. Hes too young to get it. But look at me and Ive still never gotten it.

This business of me coming to visit. What if your husband and me get squabbling? Maybe you and Dwight shoud come see me. Two weeks or some such in the sun wont cure my lungs. For the climate to help Id need to live there all the time, Ha Ha. But I don't know. Another whole winter like this one might be too much. How about I come and see you around next Christmas?

Your Pa

March the 29th

Vera,

You would think after 11 years at a job I could take my pick of vacation. But things arent meant to be, which is what the unions cant get through their skull. These people go on and on about fairness. Fairness was never a rule. The system takes no count of it. So I have to plan my visit a long ways ahead if I want to get the weeks I want. So you need to tell me whats' best at your end. When you figure in the cost of round trip train and time spent on board I would feel silly staying less than say 10 days. Can you 3 stand me that long? Around Christmas makes the most sense. But I will probably have a better chance getting 2 weeks in January.

Do you cactus eaters get the Television? Earl Simonson bought one mostly for Friday night fights, now he cant get Shirley to come away from the set. Every time he turns around shes at it. At least she doesnt growse at him so much for times at

Smalleys with me. To me its nothing but a damn fool waste. If you wanted to buy one Id say pay back that money first. Which lets you know how I feel because I never want you to pay back one penny.

Pa

10.   The Green Stone

In this darkness Dwight doesn't want to know the time of day. He wants to live in a hot room lit by a bare bulb where a man and woman argue above the hum of traffic in the night street beneath their open window. He wants to live in a black-and-white world of racetracks and narrow stairwells, alone and safe among strangers. If only he could stride down the aisle in his baggy dark blue uniform and turn off the pink light of the clock up there right next to the screen. Then all the walls would be blank, nothing to look at but the movies themselves.

Late one afternoon he goes to see his boss in his tiny office on the second floor. Kyle Brand is hunched over his typewriter banging out the schedule for September. In this hole within a larger hole, Brand keeps his sunglasses on. Over his desk a patch of light falls through one small window.

"How come we have the clock?"

"Convenience of the clientele." Brand takes off his sunglasses to examine his typing.

On the wall over Brand's desk is a poster for *Underworld, USA*, another of the thousands of movies waiting for Dwight, thousands of hours that will sit in silver cans for as long as it takes him to get around to seeing them all. The eyes of Kyle Brand, gray or no color at all, are they dying from too many movies?

There's no such thing as too many movies.

"People wander in with a couple hours to kill," the man is saying. "They need to keep track of the time."

"People should come here to watch the movies and forget everything else."

"How many people come to this place to watch the movies?"

Brand puts his sunglasses on. Dwight reads the titles for September 18 upside-down as they are typed in: *On Dangerous Ground* and *The Big Combo*. He knows Brand is right. The Drake accomodates those people of downtown Chicago who need a cheap escape from the cold, the rain, the humid heat. They come here to hide from somebody to whom they owe money. They come, as Sheffield did, to dry out. Most of them can't tell a Fritz Lang from a Preston Sturges. He wants to walk up and down the aisles poking the men who are asleep and lecturing the ones who watch blankly until everyone is alive to these words and gestures of high importance.

Mrs. Brand comes in and stands looking out the window at the people at work under yellow lights next door, filling out forms, dialing phones, at work filing their nails. Tall and angular, she towers over her husband when he sits at the typewriter. In his seven weeks working at the Drake Dwight has seen Kyle and Mara Brand in exactly this pose many times, the man at his desk, the woman gazing across at the workers next door. To Dwight Mrs. Brand looks as if she should speak with exactly the trace of a Slavic accent that she does.

"What should I do about this double dealer, Mr. Brand?"

"Double dealer?"

She turns to Dwight: "A certain gentleman steals paperbacks from the rack in front of my shop. Next day he comes in to sell the books back to me."

"And you tell him to get lost?"

She shakes her head. "I should. I tell myself, Throw this element out on Clark Street. Instead I hand over a dime and I can't even look him in the eye." She turns from Dwight as if he were the thief. "Think of someone reduced to that means of making ten cents."

"Maybe he's always wanted to make his living doing something he enjoys. Reading is what he likes best, and here's how he gets paid for it."

"And maybe," Kyle Brand says, "he's just another bum with a new angle."

"I don't know," says Mara Brand, "I think I like Dwight's idea."

From the office he walks softly on the thinning carpet to the Gallery entrance and taking two steps inside he looks around to make sure all the people here are female. "LADIES: TRY THE GAL-LERY: FOR GALS ONLY!"—so reads the Drake schedule every month. Part of Dwight's job is to check every once in a while to see that these ladies are undisturbed by male hands, by the breath of male drunks.

All is well. Five women sit in scattered seats. Two of them sleep, another mumbles too quietly to be a bother, and the other two pay close attention to Irene Dunne weeping over the death of her adopted daughter. One of the latter two women is Boils, so called by Dwight because her face is full of large round sores. She shows up every morning, sometimes before the Drake opens, and sits through at least three complete double-features. Where is home, how does she spend her nights, what job supports this habit of hers?

There is no better job for himself. Like Boils, he sees each film three times, enough to memorize the best scenes before going home. Lying awake at night he no longer recounts these movies to his grandfather but runs the best scenes through his mind, lingering over a certain exchange, a woman's face in a certain light, till the scenes merge with his dreams.

The nervewracking comedies of Sturges or Howard Hawks

offer countless treasures for his private screenings. Westerns set in a desert put him in mind of lying awake in a different bed on Arizona nights, hearing the screen door bang and bang. War movies tend to drag but usually contain at least one character or heroic sacrifice worth saving. Most of all, of course, he looks forward to the black-and-white detective movies, their continuous play of doubt and shadows. The best of these he would sit through more than three times, if that were possible.

What he can't stand are musicals, the bursting into implausible song, the endless fluttering of eyelashes. On musical days he spends as much time as he can in the lobby, vacuuming, rearranging candy bars, scrubbing the picture cases and ticket-booth window till all are thick with glass cleaner. But one day last week Brand ran a double bill of *Top Hat* and *Swing Time*, and Dwight found himself drawn inside to watch the "Never Gonna Dance" number two extra times; even today, a dozen movies later, the vision of Astaire and Rogers spinning and spinning and spinning and spinning atop the glass staircase remains, against his own will, in the boy's mind.

From the Gallery comes a shriek. Having just returned to the main floor, Dwight darts back up the stairs. A man has snuck in, crawled down a row on hands and knees, and laid his head gently in the lap of a sleepy middle-aged woman. She continues to shriek, even as the man backs away, still on all fours, a drowsy horse swinging his head. As Dwight comes forward he notes that the woman's skin is the same color as the fair-to-middling coffee he drinks every morning at the Brass Penny. He almost trips over the man. Boils turns around, her voice loud enough to be heard over Cary Grant and Irene Dunne: "Men are barred from this area. You had better get a move on, pronto."

Dwight pulls the man slowly to his feet and leads him out of the Gallery. Kyle comes out of his office and accompanies them down to the lobby and outside. In the tired air of Clark Street he hands the man one of his short black cigars. "About time," the man says, and trudges off. His smell lingers only a moment before being swallowed in the metallic filth of the Loop.

Dwight stares after him. The man is not much older than Dwight himself.

The boy arrives home to find his grandfather sitting up in his rocker, a rare vision of strength.

"I want you to quit."

Dwight shrugs. "So what do we live on?"

"My Social Security, for the little time I've got left. You better not mention money after what you let happen."

Sitting on Hazard's bed the boy studies the sweat marks on the pillow case, on the sheets. He doesn't care about his wages, he would work in the Drake for free. What he won't do is stay here watching the old man's pain, hearing his silent rage over the lost money, seven weeks' worth of rage.

"I'd go nuts if I stayed here all the time."

"Stay where you are and you will anyway. You're a prisoner there."

"Who's a prisoner? I get paid, and I like it."

"A prisoner cause your life's tied up there. You don't even hear when I say come home as one last favor."

"I know you're bad off, but you're getting by. And now I'm home every night to fix your supper. You don't need me around here every minute."

Then nobody says anything. Dwight gets up, wishing he could pull his own words down from the air and crush them in his hand.

"We need groceries," he says.

Walking to and fro in the Hi!Neighbor he hears his own

words played back and back. Getting by, bad off but, you don't need. He told Hazard to go to hell so he himself can stay locked inside a nuthouse of moving pictures.

And why not? How will it help the old man to have Dwight home all day? The poison still hangs in the air between them, not dissolved when they mutter at each other. If only Sheffield would show up at the door, wearing a clean suit and itching to talk and to listen. The boy would recite whole scenes from Ida Lupino movies, recount every one of his few memories of his mother and his one memory of his father, describe exquisitely the look on Victor Shields' face when Dwight told the fat slob, "I was gone a long time ago."

Sheffield won't show up, in a clean suit or any other, smelling of liquor or blood. On a Saturday afternoon at the Brass Penny Dwight had a last chance. He let it slip by. How many days later did the man cut his throat? Three nights after the afternoon they shook hands and Dwight said nothing. And now there is nothing but the boy coming out to the Hi!Neighbor to escape the poison hanging between himself and his grandfather, out to this place where he used to work—was it only a year ago?—where they keep the air conditioning so cold you have to move forward all the time, past the canned vegetables, canned fruit, on.

He's right. Who needs him around? I hardly eat anymore. If he does come home let him not say another word another month. This way no more grilling me for some useless truth from the past.

Next he'll start in asking me again where she's buried. When you grew up I'd tell you. Now I'm going back on my word. None of your business. Your job's to live your own life, not look at her gravestone and worry what went haywire. Nothing to change there. Nothing to learn.

"You say something?" Dwight calls.

From the bedroom, silence, then more mumbling. Dwight

goes back to humming "Town Without Pity" while he chops parsley and peels potatoes.

Griping about the food, most likely, this supper he'll keep saying he won't eat right up till I march it in and stick it under his nose. Lucky for him I learned to like to cook, otherwise he'd get TV dinners every night instead of every third or fourth.

Does he know how lucky he is?

"What brand poison you dishing up tonight?" the old man says, if not loud enough for Dwight to hear, at least loud enough to guess the words from the music of the voice.

"Meat loaf and parsley-boiled potatoes brand."

"Partly boiled potatoes? What's wrong with all boiled?"

Eventually Dwight comes to give names to all the regular patrons of the Gallery: Boils; the woman he rescued from the interloper, whom he calls Wire after the taut bone structure of her face; and three who are named for their respective favorite pastimes in the Drake: Mumbler, Weeper, and Dozer. Riding to work one morning he is startled to see Dozer get on at Belmont Avenue. She stays awake all the way down to Madison, where she and Dwight get off at opposite ends of the car. He stays far enough behind to pretend he is tailing her through the damp morning, enjoying the movement of her hips beneath her beige raincoat and the way she turns her head slightly once as if to let him know she knows he's there. By eight o'clock, when he goes up for his first Gallery check, she is already slouched low in her seat, her eyes half closed. Does she see more than a few minutes of any film?

The main floor clientele are harder to tell apart. Except for the occasional brave couple out on a date, most of them are lone men who don't do much of anything during the movies. Infrequently one or another shouts abuse or encouragement to an actor, but most of the time they sit blank and patient, staring out their days as if the Drake were a prison and each double-bill another hatch mark on a calendar ending in their own deaths. The women upstairs might have outside lives. The men seem to exist only here inside the ripe air of the main floor.

In the movie that runs through him while he rides to and from work, these men play supporting roles. The women of the Gallery, and Dwight himself, are the main characters. He is an eye so private he will not hire himself out to anyone, instead he works alone on whatever cases take his interest. A man is going around Chicago stabbing women, leaving them to die in gangways, in dead ends of alleys. The police are making routine investigations but none of them will lose sleep over the case; after all these women live alone, are survived by nobody. A series of cryptic exchanges, violent threats, anonymous phone calls at 3:45 AM, leads Dwight on a roundabout journey to the Drake. The victims have one thing in common: all frequent the Gallery. Now he spends his days and evenings at the Drake, each main floor man a suspect. One day he sees *This Gun for Hire* and realizes the woman called Dozer bears a resemblance to Veronica Lake. Of course she is older now, her blond hair carries streaks of silver, yet the connection is there. Checking back through the files he finds that each victim resembled, even if only distantly, an actress from the 30s or 40s, Carol Lombard, Rita Hayworth, Jane Greer. This woman who once looked like Veronica Lake may be the next scheduled victim. When he offers her his protection she tells him she can take care of herself but he follows her home anyway, sitting at the opposite end of the car.

The el rattles along through the middle of a winter night, its columns of lights flashing off and on in no particular relation to the starts and stops of the baritone sax on the soundtrack. The cry of the wheels could cut into the next victim's screams, but Dwight won't settle for that trick: the murders, when they happen, must happen as if in a silent film. Following Dozer down an alley, the detective will be hit on the head from behind, will imagine the murder while lying unconscious in the alley.

But the next victim is a different patron, a woman not unlike Ida Lupino in the shape of her nose and the sadness in her eyes. Now the private eye does win the trust of the woman called Dozer. Saying goodbye to her one morning he is gunned down on the front steps of her apartment building just so she can run down in her white robe and cradle him in her arms. Whose face will he see in his dying moment: Veronica Lake's? Vera Cope's?

Once, deep into *Woman in the Window*, standing at his post at the rear of the main floor, Dwight feels a tap on his shoulder. "Phone call," Brand whispers. Dwight follows him out to the ticket booth. The street is almost too bright.

"Hey, it's daytme."

"The daylight world recaptured," Brand says. "One of the many wonders given us by movies."

For the first time in months Dwight hears his grandfather's voice over the phone. It sounds stronger than in person.

"I can't get out of bed."

While Dwight is changing into his street clothes Brand stands at the Mens' Room mirror applying drops to his eyes and telling Dwight the rest of *Woman in the Window*: "The whole thing turns out to be a dream. Can you believe Lang would settle for such a silly ending?"

Puffs of milkweed drift against the windows of the el as it climbs out of the subway and rocks along, so close to the tenements fronting the tracks that Dwight can see into a hundred windows in five minutes. A hundred tableaux: a man raising his fist; two cats dreaming on a sill; one brown beer bottle at the edge of a green table. Today of all days Dwight wants to soar from the el and float through the midday heat into any of these rooms, become a watcher of someone else's slow adventure of decay. Dreaming of such escapes he almost misses the Lawrence stop, in the moment before the doors unfold back into their closed posture he leaps to the platform. On a Marlboro poster someone has painted, in huge yellow letters: REPENT AND FOLLOW SATAN.

Slowly the lukewarm tub-water rises. After he hoists his grandfather from the bed on to his shoulders he has to stop a moment, not because the old man weighs too much but because he weighs so little. Five feet ten inches tall, this old man once weighed close to two hundred pounds. Now he could be a sack of dry sticks in the boy's arms. Dwight turns and looks into the exhausted face of his burden and wants to read its thoughts.

I told you so. I told you I'm near my end.

He carries him easily through the bathroom doorway and as he bends he eases his grip slowly and lets Hazard slip into the water. The old man lies still until Dwight moves to start washing him. "I can wash myself."

The boy goes to strip the bed. Why do his arms shake? It can't be from the non-weight he has just carried. Why, when he is telling himself not to worry about the old man, does he want to clench his fists until the nails cut into his palms?

Rolling the sheets and the soiled union suit into a bundle, he calls out, "How you feeling in there?"

"How do you think it feels to crap yourself in bed and get carried on somebody's back like a cripple? In my life I never had to count on anybody. I only mooched from welfare for your ma's sake. And here I'm begging you to quit work and care for me."

"You didn't beg me. You told me what happened and I came."

The boy is frightened by the old man's unusual power to speak so many words. He hears the splash of a fist into the water.

"I been begging off you a whole year now. Just get out. If you won't quit that job, then move out, see what it's like to live alone."

"Hell," Dwight says quietly. "I know that already."

"You're damn tootin'. We both know."

The back stairs smell of coal, the truck must have come by this morning. The old man still never speaks of his years below. Last week Dwight saw an old miner's lamp in the junk shop window. If he brings that lamp home, will it make him talk about those days, or will it only remind him, as if he needed reminding, of his dying?

He crams the bundle down the incinerator and waits for the thump. Might as well burn this stuff as try to wash it, then it won't be around to make Hazard feel more ashamed. But he shouldn't feel that way. He should stop going on how he always made it on his own. Those days are finished.

If they're finished, then Dwight does have to quit. But maybe his grandfather wants to be left alone now. He said as much. Just get out.

He won't get out. He won't abandon him. But he won't take on that silence either, he won't give up his own world for that.

The heat has exhausted him. At one in the afternoon, he needs a nap. Standing still, he inhales the scent of coal dust.

Dwight can't tell what movie they are watching, he can only see the shadows of images against their faces. On the armrest between them the tub of popcorn will be full forever. Not once do they glance at each other. Taking her hand, Sheffield draws it to his mouth, never blinking. As if unaware what he's doing Sheffield licks the butter from Vera's fingertips. Slowly Vera draws Sheffield's hand to her mouth. The shadows will move across their faces forever.

Dear Mister Cope,

Enclosed you will find a camera, one of several found in the possession of my late brother Arthur Sheffield. These possessions came to me after his accident. Arthur had attached your name and address to this particular camera, apparently to send it to you as a present, which he no doubt would have done had it not been for his fall.

Although my brother and I had not been in close contact during past years I will treasure his memory, and place my faith in the Almighty that he is as peace.

Sincerely,

Mrs. Thomas Lyons

Though never struck by sunlight, even this closet is imprisoned by heat tonight. Crouched in the smell of all the clothes his grandfather hasn't worn for a year, of the old man's shoes and the cheap plastic Jesus, Dwight holds a camera in his hands.

An hour ago he owned nothing. Then he got up from his nap and checked the mail. This camera once took pictures for Sheffield, whose sister trusts he is at peace. Sheffield's finger pressed this button. Aiming the camera into the less dense darkness of the old man's room, he remembers: take a picture in the dark, any ghost in the camera's eye will come out in the picture. Where did he hear that legend? From his mother, as told by her mother. Would the ghost be Vera herself? Vera's, and Sheffield's, do they show up at the Drake on weekday afternoons and sit together with the popcorn between them? If he takes a shot of two empty seats tomorrow, will the picture reveal the two ghosts, watching?

Even this hot of a night I'd be out on the street if I could. Then why is he sitting in my closet, making a mine of this place? The walls of the mine aren't these. Down there no lizard shape in the walls, no cow's skull. No end to the dark. This dark will end, the lizard will come to my sight again. Down there no coming to light. Then why does he sit in there hardly breathing? What keeps him still?

Mara Brand's bookshop is so narrow that when Dwight stands in the middle and stretches both arms he can almost touch the books lining both walls.

"One of these days I'll be able to touch both sides at once."

Sitting behind the counter, Mara looks up at him. "On that day you'll begin reading. Starting with whatever two books you touch first, you'll have to read every book in my shop."

"I used to read a lot, mostly in the summer. *Robinson Crusoe, Last of the Mohicans, The Black Arrow*. What else? *Oliver Twist*, and a bunch of biographies, Babe Ruth, Aaron Burr, Clara Barton. Charlie couldn't believe I was reading a book about a nurse! So then to get his goat I read one on Florence Nightingale. But when I went back to school I'd lose interest. Why read books somebody else says you have to read? They drummed it out of me. But now when there's a scene in a public library, or a private eye gets led into a waiting room where the walls are lined with books I think, God there's so much to read. Or a bookstore, some great scenes have taken place in bookstores. But first I want to see a couple thousand more movies, then I can start in again on books."

She shakes her head. "The movies will make you blind first. Then you couldn't take my picture, even if I wanted you to, which I don't. I've never liked photographs. Paintings are a matter of imagination, but not photographs. The movies, either. Mister Brand and I have what do you call it, a gentleman's agreement: I don't have to see his movies and he doesn't have to read these books."

Now Dwight wishes he could take a picture of the two of

them together, with this caption: The Strangest Couple in Chicago—Each One Hates What the Other One Loves.

"How do you know you don't like movies?"

"I saw a few when we first were married. There was one, *Rome, Open City; Roma, Citta Aperta*. This film, it hurt me. There was a woman shot down in the street as she ran after her husband whom the Nazis had taken prisoner. And then another man, not this woman's husband, was tied in a chair and tortured with fire and tortured in other ways, and a priest made to watch. It was too close to real life. It hurt me. But it was too far also. If I had seen such a thing in the street or in a house I could have stopped it or died trying to stop it. But here in this film there was nothing. I felt paralyzed. I was."

While she speaks he has to restrain himself from taking a picture of the evening sun through the bookshop window against one side of her face and the hard brightness of her eyes. The books behind and above her, some of the titles in light, some in darkness, must be caught here and now. So must the light between the window and her face, between her face and the books, the counter and the ceiling. The camera wants to capture the fields of light and columns of shadow. The camera itself is afraid to leave this light.

A man and a woman are shouting at each other. Suddenly she slaps his face and without a pause he slaps hers so hard she falls down.

9:21 by the pink clock.

His mother crouched this way once when he came in from playing outside to find her and the man who must have been his father standing by her with his hands over his own face while she lay there trying to breathe. Dwight had gone inside for water and to lie safe from the desert. Like Dwight's own the man's hair was black and wavy. His face covered by his hands.

The boy went running back out into the heat, across the red field down to the clay riverbed, the dry red bed.

On the cool floor of the Wrigley Field Mens Room lay Hazard. Another boy's knees held Dwight down in the mud. Hazard's face tried to breathe, Hazard's daughter's face, the face of this actress after the actor has taken his revenge for her slap, and what revenge was Ray Cope taking when Dwight ran in from the desert, what had Vera done to make her husband knock her to the floor?

Hazard's face.

9:22. What am I doing here?

He turns from the screen. He walks upstairs to Brand's office.

"My grandfather's dying."

Brand looks up from filling out orders—November? December? Dwight wants to know the titles so two months from now he can think, If I still worked at the Drake I'd be seeing . . .

"Sorry to hear it," Brand says.

"I have to stay home and take care of him."

"Well, you lasted longer than most on the job."

"I wish I could stick it out. Things are just getting to me."

"I know. I can barely sit through these movies myself anymore. Cheroot?" Brand hands him one and the USHER WANTED sign. "Put this up on your way out, will you?"

In the locker room, changing out of his uniform, he imagines that he is changing into it, entering this dark shelter instead of leaving it behind.

"So what brings you by, Dwight? Not that you need a reason or nothing."

"Nothing special. I don't know. I quit my job today."

"From the paper?"

"No, I was—never mind about that, Tommy. What did you

mean when you said my mother was 'something'? You said, 'Christ, she was something.' "

When Tommy leans forward in his armchair, Dwight, sitting on the floor beside him, has to shield his eyes from the noonday sun through the front room window. Laughing, Tommy lifts the handle of his dark glasses and scratches with his good hand.

"I did say that, didn't I? Well, she was. Out of all the old gang she was the one who stayed friends when I came back. Of course most of the guys were overseas, but there were plenty of people around who could've been my friend. She was the one. But not only that. She wanted to make something of herself. You know she actually liked school? Grimm High, she got a kick out of going there! That's how I know she'd be proud you turned out the way you did."

"How'd I turn out?"

"I don't know. Smart. Graduating high school." He jumps up. "Georgie's home early."

Dwight, who has heard no sound of someone coming, watches Tommy walk to the front door. He opens it only a crack. "I gave at the factory."

"I'm too thirsty for this," George says. He brushes past Tommy and heads down the hall.

"Home early," Tommy says.

From the kitchen come the sounds of George finding a beer and opening it. "They gave us the afternoon so we'd have three-and-a-half days off. You too?"

"Nope," Tommy says quietly. "I just didn't feel like it today. I felt like hearing the game in the comfort of my own home. You want a beer, don't you Dwight? In this heat? Bring us two, Georgie." He sits again in the armchair. "I'll tell you, I used to be so conscientious. Years and years I'd hardly miss a day at the plant. Now I can't make myself give a fuck anymore. One of these days, who knows, they might even fire me. If they can get up the nerve."

George comes in with three bottles of Blatz, puts one in Tommy's good hand, gives another to Dwight. He seems much older than Dwight expected; though only six years older than Dwight he looks as old as Tommy, whose chubby cheeks give him a youthful look. George is tight and worn, his curly black hair growing thin.

"How you been, Dwight?"

"Strange. Things are strange these days, George."

George laughs. "You're telling me. Around here, strange is S.O.B." He turns to Tommy. "If Lucille calls tell the witch I'm sleeping it off. And try to keep the ballgame low, okay, Tom?"

Bottle of beer in hand, he disappears into the bedroom.

"He looks old," Dwight says.

"Well," says Tommy, "the man does get around."

The words of a man who gets around: Tell the witch. S.O.B.: Same Old Baloney.

"But that ain't it," Tommy continues. "He looks old from six years in the same shithole job. I'm there nineteen years, but Georgie's got no reason to settle for what I've had. Plus he's stuck in the same old flat he grew up in, with nobody left but him to take care of his brother the blind man. No wonder he chases women. He'd be better off in the army only they don't take guys with ulcers."

"They don't take guys with a heart murmur either. Not that I belong in the army anyway."

"No, you sure don't, kid," says Tommy, laughing again. "You're not exactly the type." When he takes a gulp the beer foams up and spills around the edges of his mouth. "Holy Mother, come look at me now."

Dazed by the beer, the sunlight, by Brand's cheroot and by Tommy's easy voice Dwight lies back on the floor.

"Tell you the truth," Tommy says, "I wasn't exactly the type either."

"No, you're too colorful. A couple of years ago we had to

write an essay on somebody we knew who was colorful. A guy in my class thought I'd choose my grandfather. But I chose you. You're a hell of a lot more colorful than the old man."

Tommy sits silent. Then: "I don't know. But if it means you're not the army type, I qualify."

Dwight puffs away, staring at the ceiling. What would it be like, to be the type for any particular life, to belong in the army, or anywhere? He used to belong here among all the people of Patrice Rigney's family, used to lie here on Sunday mornings staring at this same ceiling's blankness, no cracks or shapes of animals or of monsters or birds. For twenty years Tommy hasn't seen this blank ceiling nor the dust under the radiator, the stain, shaped like a fist, on the side of his armchair. The army did that. Well, the army is out, at least for Dwight. Then there's working, not as an usher but at some real job, chasing women or not, getting married or not, working.

As if to himself Tommy says, "So what's on your mind?"

Dwight studies the line of upholsterer's nails at the base of the couch. "This guy who used to try and sneak into the balcony at the movie theater. All the hoboes I had ever seen were old, or close to it. But this guy had to be in his early twenties. I thought you had to go through the mill for a big part of your life before you could hit bottom. Thinking about that man scares me."

"You won't end up like that. You're too smart."

"Maybe he was smart and left that part of himself behind on the road."

Tommy is silent. Dwight gets up. "Tommy? I guess I better get home."

"Hang on a minute."

Tommy gets up. Dwight holds his breath when Tommy turns the corner into the hall. But the man has been turning that corner in the same darkness for twenty years, has found his way down the hall to his room ever since he came home and was befriended by Dwight's mother. What did she do or say to cut through the darkness he had brought home with him from North Africa?

"Close your eyes, Dwight, and hold out your hand."

Tommy is standing so close the boy can smell his beer breath. He feels Tommy's good hand press lightly into his, and when the hand is taken away a smooth and not very heavy object has been left in Dwight's palm.

"Open?"

"Whenever."

The stone is flat, a good skimming stone, oval, about the size of a silver dollar, and the color of the lake on a summer day that's cloudy and bright at the same time.

"She gave me that rock the last time we went for a walk. I guess she wanted to give me something to remember her by, without saying she was going."

"And you kept it."

"Why not? On top of my dresser. Once in a while ma used to tell me throw it out—But what are you keeping this for, Tommy, a good luck charm? Now I've had the rock long enough. Now it's yours 'cause I put it in your hand. What do I need with it? I can't even remember what color."

"Green, Tommy. It's green."

The old man is sitting up in bed with one of his Zane Grey novels when Dwight walks in. The boy stands looking at the Arizona sagebrush on the cover, waiting for Hazard to ask him what he's doing home at one-fifteen in the afternoon.

"No game?"

"On-Deck Circle," says Hazard. "I hate all that talk."

Dwight sits in the rocker. Hundreds of afternoons, evenings, he and his grandfather have sat here or in the front room and listened to the whole broadcast, pre-game through post-game, the old man now and then talking back to whatever player, coach, manager, or front-office clown happened to be answering the same old questions.

Hazard says, "Ever since Quinlan got killed I don't like the radio guys. We should move the TV in here. Brickhouse ain't bad except when he puts away one too many Hamm's."

"You hated the TV these whole six years. Now all of a sudden you're going to watch?"

"Free country."

Dwight starts rocking slowly, drawing out each squeak as long as possible.

"What's your problem? That place get raided for harboring too many hoors?"

"I don't have a problem. I'm home because I quit my job."

Hazard looks up. He looks again at the page, closes the book, and says, "Nice going."

"Hazard. Grampa. Tell me something."

A question. A question about his mother. My daughter.

"How could she teach me to read? I thought I learned in school."

The old man shakes his head. "You knew."

"But how? She wasn't a teacher, she was just my mother."

"I don't know how she did it."

"Then tell me something. Tell me what you do know."

∆ ∆ ∆

May 2nd

Dear Papa,

I'm sorry I didn't write back as soon as you wrote and said you're going to visit but things have been a little hectic lately and for some reason I assumed if you ever came it would be in the summer although of course winter makes more sense for you. Plan what seems right. Dwight and I are looking forward to it already.

You know your joke about moving here for good is not all that funny. You couldn't pick a better place, all this wonderful air, Doctor Crandall says so, too.

Love, Vera

May the 18th

Vera,

Went ahead and got a train ticket to get there on January the 10th. They told me Centinelas the nearest place to Hobart on the line. I can be there close to 10 days before heading back. And still get a days rest before starting back in at the plant. How does this sound from your end?

Pa

PS. I dumped that doctor Mejian. He started telling me work less hours (at my age) and to cut down on my White Owls. A doctors a doctor I finely realizd.

June the 25th

Dear Vera,

Found that old telegram with the wrong time of Dwights birth again. Didnt you tell me they got it all wrong? Anyway it reminded me his birthdays coming up. Heres a little money order to get him something with. Maybe hes' old enough now for his first baseball mitt. But you and your husband know best. Now that summer has hit Ive been out to Wrigley a few times.

As if I had to tell you. I get a kick out of seeing the Giants whove got this colored rookie in center who they say hell be the greatest one of these days. Although Jackie R. is still the best, colored or what have you.

Hope you havent run into more problems money wise. Let me know. Also if my plans suit you.

Love, Pa

11. The Day After Labor Day

The first one: of his last pair of shoes on the sunlit floor with the striped radiator shadows crossing his shoetops. Then, his boots, not the long-gones he wore into the mine but his factory workboots sitting there in the same spot. Third, the boots off to one side casting their shadows on the shoes in the center. Last, the miner's lamp on the bureau shining down on his shoes lying with the soles sticking up. I didn't make this one clear enough to show the specks of blood on the right instep and there's no way to tell the splotch on the left sole is his own blood off the Wrigley Field Mens Room floor.

Don't they look at the photographs they develop? When I went to pick them up this morning the man in the shop didn't even stare at me like I was weird.

He's there. Here. Why not gone?

In the time it took to pick up these photographs and pin them on his walls I could have gotten him to the hospital.

He doesn't want to die around strangers but here in this room without some doctor telling him how to go about doing it.

Can you say someone is growing smaller? What's left of him keeps gathering tighter around his bones while I sit here in his rocker, get up and take away his pan, play with this pack of Camels. The matches say SEND IN TODAY FOR OUR COURSE IN ELECTRONICS AND BE YOUR OWN BOSS

IN SIX MONTHS! Another life to picture and then discard while I wait for him to speak.

When I can't fall asleep in the rocker I stretch out beside him and inhale the mine every time he tries to breathe out deep.

Could have burned them. Should have. Now he'll find them, read them. Unless he's made to swear he won't look at a word. Burn them instead. Swear.

Turn on the game in the middle and it's like the radio holds knowledge of everything you've missed, exactly how the Cubs are behind in this one. But they've done better this year than any since the old man started taking the little slob I used to be to Wrigley Field. As soon as I start thinking they may not be worth every minute of my attention they start playing what for them is superhuman baseball.

They keep announcing names of different groups of people who've come out to the game. If I listen long enough I'll hear, "Also at the ballpark today—Raymond Cope, that lonesome traveling man who just checked into Chitown after a good long stretch of road time."

Can he tell these are the Braves? Can he tell there's a game? His eyes stay open as if wanting to learn everything from the ceiling he hasn't learned already.

The worst thing is I'm starting to like it here. Sure I've taken care of him this past year and more but this is different, nothing *but* taking care of him now, and instead of wanting him to die or even get well this part of me wishes he'd stay sick forever so I'd never have to decide to leave this place behind. When I was a kid the hard decisions were things like whether to send away for the Charles Atlas Bodybuilding Course or Joe Weider's Crash-Weight Formula #7, and it wasn't too tough to choose neither one: the money wasn't there. Now even after meeting up with disaster in the alley I've still got the hundred bucks I was talked into saving by Joan Fontaine. And then you've got an employable skill Sheffield said. Once the old man goes there's no excuse to stay where I am.

It doesn't matter what I wish. He won't keep being sick forever, or another day.

Gone long ago. Should have been. Let this end happen by its lonesome. Not with him around in the bright of day. Bright like Alice liked, like Vera. Should have taken her to Wrigley to see the light. She would have understood.

"I couldn't find her." Almost too quiet to hear.

Sky that day burlap. Color of the blanket night of yellow stars.

At his voice I turn off the radio and sit by him: "You couldn't find who? Grampa. You mean my mother?"

He nods. The room this quiet again.

"Vera got lost? When?"

Nods again.

"Did she have a lot of boys after her, Grampa? Probably frightened them off, too quiet and mysterious. They took her for cold. In the factory she got in trouble for not being friendly enough, they took her silence for some kind of challenge, they made her out to be a rebel. But she ran away with him on an impulse, like I might have run away if you hadn't gotten sick. Not to hurt you or prove something, just up and left."

No sign.

"Glass of water."

Every sound so distant. They brought me water. The blanket felt like burlap. But the sky black, yellow starlit. "Rackham, Jessup, Tiberi, Dix, Gleason, Carson—no, Floyd." Kid must wonder who these names. Seth down there too and Lemuel. And Pa. Only me lifted up. Heard Jessup's woman crying far away. But she's a lot of women, near me, some with torches. *Boys too and old men. Lights drifting forward to stare.* "Broke my arm, Seth. And leg or just ankle. Pa, I cracked a couple ribs." *Don't laugh, hurts too much when. Wish I was enough in shock to free me knowing I'm the only one lifted up. Saved.* "Feels like burlap. Taste like." *Then came a waiting for a wagon. Torches, their eyes. Now this boy over me to say something he can follow, remember, live by. Every mistake of movement sending the names right through me,* "Dix, Cargill, Floyd," *Gone this one, that one, gone Pa.* "And Lem, Seth." *But me under a blanket for a wagon to fix me so I can go back down alone when I'm fixed.* "Yellow lights came out to the sky." *Before Alice, before I knew the kid's grandmother the stars watched me wait. Knives in my ribs when I laughed at their names. But the burlap water mine, the ribknives.* "Mine." *Then a sound wagon wheels made. Loaded on, every jolt a new knife. Do what I please. Close my eyes to listen the wheels or open to all the yellow stars. Mended I'll go back down, come out alone.* "Before I met your grandma." *How all this light if the earth fell on each of us? Lie still the end comes in all our own good time. Pa's among the faces lifting me. But he's pinned below. Ma died of plain exhaustion here above but he dies below so his face in the flickering eyes to hold me safe. To live out how many days? Father a daughter who bore a son and died her way. Come to lie in this bed a year awaiting the weight will press out a last breath. The weight fell on my arm, ankle, side. Over the years the other grows in you. Rise from the death room below and end up under this other air.*

Nothing about Vera but at least he spoke, at least I could follow some of his words.

"Grampa? Yesterday was Labor Day, remember me telling you?"

Not even a sign of anger. He used to call it a bad joke—Any day set aside to honor us should be crossed off the year, it would take whole lifetimes to pay back us working fools for all we've been through.

"Preacher. No preacher. Doc." After all this time he wants a doctor. "No doc. No preacher."

Who was about to send for either of those people? Not me. I never even knew a preacher since the Centinela priest who wasn't so bad from far away standing up there at the front of the church but in his office the way he smiled made me feeze inside. Why'd she take me in with her? He patted my head and smiled. Father Somebody. Smile for the father.

Not my father.

Aunt Sissy was there too. Smile for the father.

Was that the day? After we came out from his room did we drive to Phoenix? Some day the title will come to me when I'm trying to think of something else or I'll see the same movie again and in the middle of some scene, nothing more than a man and a woman talking over coffee, I'll know I've seen this before and when. This was the first.

Or maybe never remember.

Even his whistle is dying, without him telling me where my mother got lost.

Where I went wrong, I never slapped you around. Get as far as lift my hand, then the sight of your mother hits me. "That time." Caught her stealing my pennies. "Our own to buy dinner with. Let her have it twice." Hard. Only have to see her face again stunned and I can't bring my hand down on you. For a second it stops being my own. By then you get out of my sight till the being mad passes. But what does a kid learn if he grows up never getting walloped? Nothing. "You never." At least Vera learned to not steal. Other faces of hers. Nights she'd read out on the couch. Went off into her own world. "By her face." Could tell by her eyes. Never saw the like in a girl or a boy, she loved school. Who was I to make her quit? Later I wanted to tell her, "Go back." You can go back now. She could. "Now the war's done." I won't stand in your way. She's got other ideas. Look at her eyes. She had other plans. Back before. That other day she went off somewhere into some other world. Wouldn't go with me to the Cubs. "Holiday." Wanted to take her to see Billy Herman, Phil Cavaretta. "Those names." Why not take the girl just once? "Dying for you to ask her." No. She said no. "I'm going down to the Loop today." She went her way, I went mine. Under a burlap sky. "You go to the ballgame, I'm going to the picture show today. Lost."

Now it's as if he draws himself together, not the growing smaller but a strengthening, his eyes almost focused on me. "Lost," again. "Got home from the game, she's gone. Evening. Walk back down the el station meet her coming. No luck. Sky turning burlap again. Never should let her go downtown by her lonesome. Thirteen years old. Stick close to home. She's got other plans. Try the schoolyard, city pool. Almost dark, nothing. Walked all the way to the beach without meaning to. Almost deserted. But she's there. By herself by the water standing. Where the hell, where the hell have you? Those eyes of hers, blind or barely look at me. Blind or in her other world. Never told me why not straight home. Or what picture show. Never a word."

That was your mother.

Which picture show? Nineteen thirty-eight, thirty-nine. She didn't want to go to the baseball game, she rode down to the Loop and saw, and saw—*Camille.* And fell in love for the first time, not just with Garbo, not just with Marguerite, but both at the same time. She had never known such beauty could exist, a woman could live such a life. When Marguerite vowed to make her love hate her, Vera wanted to turn her back, knowing she couldn't stand to see that happen. But she also knew it would come out right. Didn't movies always turn out just right? And when she died in her love's arms she didn't want to have to go home again ever. She walked around the Loop, she rode the train home seeing none of it, and then she walked toward the lake instead of the flat where she and her grandfather—father, my grandfather, her father—tried to live.

This place. Him here waiting for her. Me here now, both of us, waiting for him.

But it would be too easy to walk right into the lake. Instead she wanted to walk along its shore till she came to the edge of the world, to anything but the life she knew.

Then her father came and found her.

A story about Vera. Behind his words lies the part he can't ever make me see, his vision of her on the beach, that part is his alone. From here beside her father I could take a picture of her picture, but would it tell me something I don't already know or imagine? What photograph could make me remember her teaching me to read? Or tell me who took this one of her standing against the fence? The man I'll find in the hotel room, in Sheffield's mind. Or he married again, stuck around this time, never knowing he was a widower not a bigamist, raised a slew of my half-brothers, half-sisters. But he has no face. This man dying in his bed took my father's face and made it never exist except bent over his wife in the kitchen, hidden by his hands, on a day so hot I recall it from all the desert days I lived through. She's the face I know, small smile, the smell and touch I think I can still feel sometimes if I shut out everything else. She'd be thirty-six, but never, and the older I get the younger my mother looks. In a year I'll be as old as she was when her kid was born.

Back before. Your mother and me in the cold room. In the waiting for Alice to finish. After Lem who would have been a son named for his uncle. After three days waiting I saw Vera bend her mouth to Alice's. My daughter drew the life out of her mother. While the light went out from

Alice's eyes. Now Dwight bends over me, his mouth open to mine. Taking in what's left of breath. Or pulling the fire from these lungs. Baptism by. But I'm nothing without this fire so he must be killing me. But he sits in the rocker again, he can't be standing here to draw out life or pain. But neither could Vera. Dreamed in a room down by the slaughteryard, dreamed in this hot room. Get out you hick trash. Mrs. Angle. Angel. Engle. First you come in with the consumption or whatever, then your wife ups and dies right in my house. Won't have you in my rooms anymore. "Hick trash." Alice had gone through her first year high school, me into the seventh grade. To Mrs. Angle we were hick trash. For your little girl's sake I would have let you stay. But now you went and let your missus die on my property. Didn't you trash ever hear of a hospital? "A body gets too close to gone." To bother. Me here now—no doc, no man of the cloth. Neither would Alice. "Don't plague me with that talk." Whenever I'd mention God, not that the name crossed my lips often. I could mostly take him or leave him so I guess he wasn't God. Even last winter. Thought I'd found Him again but didn't last. For the better. Not sneaky this way, meet him head on with no pretending. How did that talk ever help your brother or your father in the mine? she'd ask. If Dwight was to get out the plastic Jesus now I'd hide my eyes.

Take a long shot of the lunch counter at Woolworth's and she will show up, the ghost of a teenage girl going crazy from her summer job. Fine employment for a young person starting out in the world. After Woolworth's working in the war plant must have been an improvement, at least there she got to save some of her pay for bonds.

Another picture then, after Woolworth's: the alley behind the Drake where I lost them.

A set of pictures: the lake late on a summer evening to see if she'd appear by the water's edge. The lake at six-thirty on a winter morning, in the middle of any night but a moonless.

Call Judie to come over and step into my boudoir to see my

distinguished black-and-white studies of the silver surface of the lake. Come see these pictures from a camera left me by a man who did himself in. Jiri Jarosic, the Girl in White, my father's hotel room: Judie might get these tales the way the Girl in White herself understands how the man and woman behave in a certain Nicholas Ray movie. Judie might let these stories, these pictures, be a kind of persuasion.

And what could I give her after? She's probably left for college by now anyway. Send the pictures, then, Lake Michigan, Woolworth's, the Drake: In case you're already homesick here are some lovely sights of the old home town, and you don't even have to see the ghost to enjoy them. A different kind of courtship from how he courted her, whatever that was— flowers, chocolates? Not likely. Not Raymond Cope.

Let him sit there, camera in his lap. Waiting for pictures of the corpse. Not a word. I thought having a boy would be different. But by the time I got a chance at one, too tired. If only Vera'd been a son. Dwight came too late is all. Hogwash. I had no business doing this. Daughter, grandson, no difference. And now it's done what have I left him? Shoeshine kit. A few baseball yarns. Bundle of letters he'll find when I'm gone. What should I have left him? Everything. A grandfather who had lived a different life. But was there a time I could have said No? How early? The day I went back down after they mended me? Or the first day down—can a fourteen-year-old boy say No? Or the day you're born? Set on a course. Say No, what happens then? Vera chose another life, in the end said No to it all. Your mind goes in circles till you look forward to an end where the mind might rest. No more counting Whys and Why Nots. I should have left him a life where you don't have to count Ones. Whys. "More."

And her. Three years I didn't write. Or four. What if I had? Maybe no doctor, no drugs and liquor. A different life. All it took, a letter now and then from her father. But a stranger, she ran away to be more of one. Turn into the desert, another state. The two thousand miles between us. She sent a picture of the state she lived in. The Arizona Stranger by Vera Harker. But women don't write Westerns. A woman lives for her child. Till something goes wrong. I could have kept her on the right course. All it would take is everything. I want to carry her home from the beach. These days I've still got the strength.

In the end all I did was bury her.

But I won't take a picture of Hazard, not now, not after. His shoes, boots, the miner's lamp. Not himself which is all he has left.

He says. "She's not at Rosemont."

"What?"

"South Side. Far, where I wouldn't always be going to see. Papers in the closet."

Now you know where she is. Go see her whenever you please.

Tomorrow I can ride the el and the bus and bring her flowers.

I won't. What's a grave, and why have I always wanted to see hers? The grave will be the same as her picture, same as the green stone, things, one step, two steps removed from her. Leave them be.

In twenty years I might ride across Chicago, almost a middle-aged man, stand half an hour by her name and then go home. In the meantime, concentrate on women still alive. How else can they surprise you, Judie at the party or the way Marie Walsh played stickball as good as me and tasted of peach cobbler?

From Arizona she wrote letters. Now something has got to be done with them. People do what they know is good, sometimes. The yellow stars came out to watch the torches. Her friends took care of the boy, before his grandpappy got there. After his mother turned away. Asking nothing in return, her old friends. The crazy goodness of some people. How does it stand up against all the reasons for not bothering to try? Good, sometimes. Or Patrice saving out clothes for the boy, bringing cakes and such, letting

him stay Saturday nights. She helped me raise him. Less wild. Did me
kindnesses of her own, here, a few high hot summer days. Knocked at the
back door while I read a letter. He must be told not to read her words. A
woman dying to turn away. This boy doesn't need any more such words.

His finger so thin and white I can barely see it against the
sheet points at the bureau, at her.

"Letters." Pointing down, his whole hand motions, down.

"Letters."
The one word. No strength for more. What will stop him reading them
now?

In his bottom drawer under a red flannel shirt and a belt
almost frayed through, on top of a union suit with most of its
buttons gone, this bundle: envelopes not as long but as yellowed
as the one that held the bonds. Her signature there the same
hand as *Hazard Harker* and this address and *Vera Cope, Hobart,*
Arizona across these envelopes. What's he want these for now,
to read himself to sleep for good?

At the bottom of the bundle, a piece of pink paper folded
three times. Her writing still. My name. Her words.

"For Dwight," he reads out loud. "Hawk motionless—." Reads the
rest silent. Turns it over, blank, looks to me. No sign here. No strength for
other words. Only the ones in his hand. He reads again to himself. —train
whistle—when you outgrow this sweater—with you anyway now no
matter—Looks to me again. Imagining I can tell him what he needs to
know.

"She left this behind?"
I can't even nod. No need to.

Ran away. Taught me to read. One summer worked at
Woolworth's. Forced to quit high school to defend her country.
Some bonds were left behind, for her son. So quiet she made

people think she was cold or mad or up to something. She fell in love with Garbo, with Camille. Ran away with a soldier. And killed herself, now.

Let in some air.

And killed herself.

Let the two of us breathe, in the wavy heat this woman's words bring down.

Too many letters here to read at once. Rest them under her stone's weight to hold them in place against the wind.

She loved to air out our place. Light and light wind pouring in. Till my own sight ran to meet the light in my wife's. That came later. First yellow lights in black sky. Torches, eyes. Come to raise me from the dead room.

"Lift me up."

Lighter even than the day I carried him to the tub. This time I don't have to sling him over my shoulder, fireman style, but can hold him in my arms like a cat or a baby.

Lift you up to where?

To the window.

One more afternoon in that street, Grampa, no different to them down there from any other.

So light now I could hold you here for hours, a long envelope, a sack full of weeds, pebbles, water, and your last breathing.

If you wanted me to.

Lay me down again so some kind of peace can fall down on me. The light came back to Alice's eyes in the last minutes of our waiting. You imagine it did to let that same peace, the end of counting, save you now.

For you, no such peace. Only the boy, wind, this room's quiet. Some Chicago room where sunlight turns the waiting to a dust common to my stillborn son and me.

Our stillborn.

Common to my first son, ours, second son, me.
Daughter, wife, here, with me. More.
A common wind, common dust.
More.
With me now, common to us.

"More."

Three twenty-six. Pete Runnels, American League Batting Champion, 1960: .326.

No. A man just died.

No. My grandfather who used to be a young man remembering himself a boy.

There are people to be called, to announce the passing of nobody they ever heard of. To say it's over, the slow whistle, the close to unhearable sounds of his fingers opening and closing along the edge of the sheet. To say all that's left is the window shade sucked up into the frame by a wrongway wind.

You have to close a person's eyes.

Then open more windows, the hall, my room, so the wind moves in other ways. Letters against her stone. I'll be with you anyway. She'll never show up, though, in any picture I take. No part of her life is portrayed by an actress. Her touch is only what I imagined I could feel one Saturday lying down on my bed which used to be hers. Her touch is only her dying, Sheffield's, the old man's dying, his stories of the dying of his wife, their unborn son, their stillborn son.

How many times will I wish I hadn't read her note? If I find him I will show him. Eight by twelve hotel room, winter afternoon. When I find him her note will rest in my heart's pocket.

Yesterday I packed. Only add the camera, her letters, I'm gone.

What I see: Hazard Harker, who has stopped growing smaller; pictures of his shoes; her snapshot. A room's worth of open windows. Trees, buildings, patches of sky. My own hands, dialing the phone.

What I don't see: the boots he wore into the mine. Her. Myself.

My own shoes carry me to the door.